# SHARING THE WONDER OF BIRDS WITH KIDS

# SHARING THE
# WONDER
## OF BIRDS
## WITH KIDS

LAURA ERICKSON

ILLUSTRATIONS BY KATHRYN MARSAA

**Pfeifer-Hamilton**
Duluth, Minnesota

Pfeifer-Hamilton Publishers
210 West Michigan
Duluth MN 55802-1908

218-727-0500
http://www.wholeperson.com/~books
E-mail: phbooks@wholeperson.com

*Sharing the Wonder of Birds with Kids*

Printed in the United States of America

10   9   8   7   6   5   4   3   2   1

Editorial Director: Susan Gustafson
Graphic Design: Jeff Brownell
Manuscript Editor: Kathy DeArmond-Lundblad
Cover photos: Dudley Edmundson

Library of Congress Cataloging-in-Publication Data
Erickson, Laura, 1951–
      Sharing the wonder of birds with kids / Laura Erickson.
      208 p. 23 cm.
      ISBN 1-57025-129-0
      1. Birds.    2. Birds—Study and teaching—Activity programs.
   I. Title
QL673.E74  1996
598—dc20                                          96-10141
                                                  CIP

This book is dedicated to Arthur Borkowski,
my fifth grade teacher, who taught me to open my eyes
without closing my heart.

# TABLE OF CONTENTS

# INTRODUCTION

Why should children learn about birds?

Of all wildlife, birds are the most accessible and abundant and the easiest to learn to identify, so birds provide a natural starting point for environmental education. Their beauty, song, migration routes, and long-standing importance to humans provide a magical bridge into lessons in art, music, geography, science, language arts, reading, history, and even math.

Even more important, these vivid and vivacious expressions of the natural world appeal to hearts and minds like little else. Studying them enriches children's lives in countless ways, helping their souls to soar above this increasingly urbanized world.

A friend of mine who runs educational programs at a university field station told me he's worked with inner city children who are bewildered and frightened on their first walks into even small woodlots. These children never saw a full-grown tree before coming to the field station—the outdoor boundaries of their day-to-day lives had been limited to the concrete walk between fenced-in school playground and locked-up tenement home. Even suburban and rural children who have easy access to field and forest may spend more time watching television indoors than they do playing outside.

I was a city girl from Chicago. When I was very young, I spent hours looking out our apartment window at pigeons flying in the sky high above the grimy city. When we moved to a blue-collar suburb, I treasured the neighborhood robins, cardinals, and sparrows. I never noticed crows, starlings, swifts, or other birds that were certainly around, and no one pointed them out to me. The only grown-up I knew who noticed birds was my grandpa, who had pet canaries. When I was four or five, he gave me *The Little Golden Stamp Book of Birds*. It was my greatest treasure, and I was heartbroken when one day I left it outside at nap time and a sudden downpour ruined it. By second grade, I had memorized the bird entry in our family's ancient encyclopedia—the B volume opened automatically to the bird section because I read it so often. The pictures were black-and-white, leaving the colors to my imagination. I never dreamed that I could go out and see any of these beautiful creatures in the real world outside of books. My mother, who was a girl during World War II, told me that only soldiers, spies, and peeping toms owned binoculars. No one told her, or me, that every kind of bird in the zoo could be found flying wild and free in a real place somewhere in the world. No one told us that birds of every color of the rainbow lived in or migrated through our own neighborhood or that the only tool I needed to identify them was a field guide. I didn't know such a book existed.

Many people learn about nature on their own, but I lacked the background and the vision to figure out how to find and identify wild birds without help. My brother raised a variety of breeds of homing pigeons, but I didn't realize that they were all the same species as city pigeons. When I saw a Blue Jay at Lake Geneva in Wisconsin (I recognized it from my stamp book), I thought I must be in true wilderness. A flock of assorted, colorful warblers flitting through our maple tree one spring morning "must be someone's escaped canaries," my mother explained, and I took her at her word.

When I was a high school student, I once found a dead Ovenbird in downtown Chicago, although at that time I couldn't identify it. It was tiny, olive-brown with a snow-white underside dotted with black on the breast, an orange crown outlined in black, and perfect white rings around its eyes. I was struck by its loveliness and the mystery of how such a delicate avian gem came to die in a city devoid of beautiful birds. A few years later, my mother-in-law gave me a pair of binoculars and a Peterson field guide for Christmas. Miraculously, the first page I opened to showed the Ovenbird. The thrill of recognition and the realization that, come spring, living, breathing Ovenbirds would return to woods right around Chicago changed my life forever.

I read the Peterson and Golden guides cover to cover and then Joseph Hickey's *A Guide to Birdwatching*. These books inspired me and gave me something more important than information—a framework for organizing facts so they made sense. I began to understand how scientists classify birds, how various species are related, how each species has unique needs that can be met only in certain habitats, and why some places are rich in birds while other places are poor. When I discovered the Field Museum of Natural History's publication, *Chicagoland Birds: Where and When to Find Them*, and the Michigan Audubon Society's *Enjoying Birds in Michigan*, I had all the tools I needed, and my mind became a sponge, soaking up information from other birders, books, and my own observations. I spent whole days at a local arboretum and woodlot, sometimes mustering the courage to speak to other people wandering about with binoculars. Some were too arrogant to be helpful, but others—some experienced and some as new to birds as I—became friends and companions on my journey through this new world. I took two university ornithology classes and discovered Michigan Audubon Society field trips. My universe expanded right before my eyes.

The more I learned about birds, the more aware I became of them in other contexts. Teaching elementary school gave me countless opportunities to infuse bird study into lessons that ostensibly had nothing to do with birds, from weights and measurements in math to color and form in art and aerodynamics in science. I discovered that many English words and expressions have avian origins, and I brought some of that knowledge into language arts. I collected bird jokes, stories, poems, and pictures. My students associated me with birds and, I think, enjoyed seeing an adult with such a passionate avocation. My deepest hope is that, even if they've forgotten me, some are nurturing their own passionate life interests in part because of my example.

My love for birding has taught me a valuable truth: what ignites any fever for learning comes from deep within. Wise parents and teachers don't force-feed information, nor do they point out where every piece of a puzzle is supposed to fit. Kindle children's interest, then help the curious find answers by themselves so they will feel ownership of their knowledge. Give children the joy and pride of discovering treasure themselves.

In *The Wizard of Oz*, Dorothy's long, dangerous adventure with a Scarecrow, Tin Man, Lion, Wizard, Bad Witch, and Good Witch taught her one simple lesson: she didn't need to search far beyond the rainbow to find happy little bluebirds—they were right there on her Kansas farm all along. Glinda could have told her that at the start, but then would Dorothy have so embraced the truth? Her search for the way home, with all the mishaps and joys of the quest, is what makes her story resonate. If we grown-ups want children to share our love for birds, we must hold ourselves in check as Glinda does, giving the children space to make their own discoveries. The background information I provide in this book is for you, to give you knowledge and confidence. Some of this information you will certainly impart to kids directly, but some you may want to hold in reserve, giving kids the opportunity to make their own discoveries. The destination is more valued when the journey is filled with joy and wonder. That is the secret of good teaching.

Throughout this book, my aim is to give grown-ups both the information and the inspiration to make bird study with children magical and exciting. Studying wild birds outdoors provides unforgettable and irreplaceable experiences, and I've given specific techniques for making field study, whether with your own child or with larger groups, successful. But I don't focus only on identification, natural history, and biology. Birds are an integral part of human culture as well as the natural world, providing rich and joyful learning experiences completely unrelated to life science.

The many kinds of birds and the countless ways to approach their study made it impossible for me to produce a straightforward yet all-encompassing "how-to" manual. I include specific activities and bird-study techniques, but each adult reading this book will have a unique set of interests, objectives, creative talents, and styles, so I emphasize ideas which I hope will serve as springboards for you to develop your own personally satisfying approach to sharing birds with children.

Some school teachers limit bird study to a one- or two-week unit because of curriculum constraints. Naturalists often see groups of children for only one or two half-day sessions. I hope these teachers will find information, activities, and suggestions to make this brief study exciting and memorable. Other teachers have more flexible schedules and may plan short or long lessons throughout a school year. They may also have opportunities to capitalize on teachable moments, for example, rescheduling math when a flock of Broad-winged Hawks is circling right outside the window.

Parents, grandparents, and birding mentors are luckiest of all. Without detailed plans, they can gently weave birds into their children's lives during breakfasts looking out the window, family trips to a park or beach, vacations, tree climbing adventures in the backyard—the possibilities are endless. I hope this book inspires you to make your bird-study time with children, whether it is formal or informal, whether it lasts for a single day or an entire childhood, into a memorable string of moments filled with insight, magic, and love.

# 1

# THE
# MAGIC
## OF BIRDS

The beauty, flight, innocence, and intense life force of birds stir the human soul like nothing else. Fairy tales and myths of childhood often revolve around birds: the goose that laid the golden eggs, Chicken Little, the ugly duckling who turned into a swan, the little birds that ate the crumbs that Hansel and Gretel dropped to mark their way home. Donald and Daisy Duck, Huey, Dewey, and Louie, Woody Woodpecker, Roadrunner, Daffy, Tweetie, Heckyl and Jeckyl—imaginations run wild when birds are the inspiration. And birds feed our spiritual souls as well, flying heavenward like our hopes and aspirations. Small wonder that angels are portrayed with feathered wings.

Tiny babies notice and are charmed by birds. My daughter Katie, at nine months, practiced walking by pulling herself up to stand at the living room window sill, and was so delighted with two Blue Jays that flew in every morning and afternoon to take peanuts at the window feeder that her second word, after "mama," was "boo jay." In the Disney classic *Bambi*, the little fawn's first word is "bird." Disney versions of many fairy tales gain resonance and loveliness by using woodland creatures, especially birds, as supporting characters, from the mice and birds sewing Cinderella's gown to the owl, squirrels, and songbirds dancing with Sleeping Beauty and the crows that teach Dumbo to fly. These creatures are hardly realistic portrayals of

1

**House Sparrows**

When House Sparrows gather together at dusk, all cheeping, what are they saying? Might they be talking about how their day went or telling bedtime stories?

real species, and the flight of Disney birds defies the laws of aerodynamics, yet their endearing qualities are endlessly pleasing to children and many adults, and they open young hearts and minds to lovely possibilities in the real world of nature.

Children don't need grown-ups in order to discover birds, but we can help open their eyes to the wide array of birds in their lives and encourage them to appreciate the value, fun, and beauty of birds. Point out birds as you notice them—outside the window, in the backyard or school playground, along roads and highways. Listen together to bird songs. Tiny children will be charmed to hear you whistle a conversation with your neighborhood cardinal. Grow plants that are attractive to birds, and set up feeders near your windows so children can enjoy wild birds in their own backyards.

Look for birds indoors, as well. On birthdays and holidays, see how many birds appear on greeting cards. Cardinals are a favorite Christmas card bird, perhaps because of their vivid red plumage, yet Turkey Vultures are not, despite their bright red heads and the fact that they like to eat dead turkeys on Christmas, too. Why do you suppose people don't put vultures on greeting cards? To intrigue kids, ask questions, then together search for answers.

What cars are named for birds? Can you find other products with bird names? Which of these names are fitting, and which aren't? What sports teams have bird names and mascots? How does the Toronto Blue Jay logo differ from a real Blue Jay? Why do athletes choose birds as symbols? Might it be because of a bird's speed, agility, beauty, grace, feistiness, or fierceness? Why are some birds chosen more than others?

Some bird names conjure images completely different from the birds themselves. The Common Nighthawk, unlike a real hawk, is gentle and quiet, a dainty flier, so utterly defenseless against predators that when an enemy approaches all the nighthawk can do is hiss and fly away. Nighthawks eat only while airborne, catching and swallowing whole insects in their capacious mouths. If a succulent moth walked right past a sitting nighthawk, the bird could do little more than stare longingly and maybe open its mouth wide hoping the moth would walk in. Long ago, Europeans nicknamed the night-hawk family "goatsuckers" because their wide mouths seemed just the right size and shape for sucking goats dry. Do you think sports teams would name themselves the "Nighthawks" if the players knew about real nighthawks?

What popular characters on TV and in comics are birds? On *Mr. Rogers' Neighborhood*, one character in the Neighbor-hood of Make Believe is X the Owl. Another is King Friday's bird, Troglodytes Aedon, whose name is also the scientific name of the House Wren.

If there's no way to determine the answer to a question, encourage kids to guess. How do you think the Nintendo com-pany came up with the design for Mario's "Koopa-Troopas," which look like turtles but sometimes have bird wings? How might Charles Schulz have come up with the idea for Woodstock? I wondered about that, so I wrote him a letter. He responded, "Comic strip inspiration happens so gradually that it's virtually impossible to explain. One thing leads to another and some-thing finally happens. It took me twenty years to learn to draw Woodstock so that he was a good character." If not even the creator of a cartoon character understands how he got his ideas, kids obviously can use their imaginations to guess.

Look for birds in books. In picture books, small children will find birds such as Richard Scarry's songbirds, Sandra Boynton's turkeys, and Dr. Seuss's Mayzie, the lazy bird who talks Horton the Elephant into hatching her egg. Many poets, from Ogden Nash and Emily Dickenson to Jack Prelutsky and Aileen Fischer, write about birds. Older children will find refer-ences to birds in all kinds of stories, and if they pay attention, they may even notice that some of the expressions we use in everyday language originated with birds. An *auspicious* event was foretold by looking at bird entrails in an ancient practice

**What commonplace objects are decorated with birds?**
Look at napkins, curtains, wall paper, a flag pole, lamps, postage stamps, stuffed animals, refrigerator magnets, wrapping paper, coffee mugs, cookie cutters, jewelry, playing cards— birds can be found just about everywhere. Browsing through a home appliance catalog, I've even found a loon sink and toilet.

**Bird names**

Ornithologists have standardized the common names of birds as well as the scientific names. In ornithological literature (and this book), the complete bird name is always capitalized, but shortened names aren't. We call our mockingbird the Northern Mockingbird to distinguish it from its relatives. In dictionaries and literature you'll find bluejay or blue-jay, but ornithologists refer to the species as the Blue Jay. The shortest proper names of North American birds are the Ruff and the Sora; the longest are the Northern Beardless-Tyrranulet and the Northern Rough-winged Swallow.

called *auspice*. The expression *at one fell swoop* originated as a falconry term. Grown-ups and kids can look up birdy words in the index of *Bartlett's Familiar Quotations* to find a wide variety of literary references to birds.

**Birds help humans in practical ways**

As children learn about birds, they will also learn about history, culture, geography, and many of the sciences. Wing feathers from birds were fashioned into the quills used to write the Declaration of Independence and the Constitution of the United States. Even though birds don't provide writing implements in this modern world of pens, pencils, and word processors, they still do provide us with food and warmth. Every year, more than 8 billion domestic chickens are raised in the world for their eggs, meat, and feathers. Domestic turkeys, ducks, and geese are also grown by the billions. Domestic geese in China provide Chinese people with food and Americans with most of the feathers that fill our down jackets, sleeping bags, and quilts.

Birds help us stay healthy and safe. For example, laboratories use viruses raised in live chicken eggs to produce influenza vaccines. Miners once kept canaries as pets for companionship and song, and also because, like all birds, canaries are highly susceptible to poisons. When dangerous gases seeped into a mine, the canary's death warned the workers to get out fast, saving their lives.

Birds do more than make us comfortable and safe—they also make our lives more enjoyable. Paintings and carvings of birds beautify our homes, and feathers often decorate our hats. Native wild American birds can no longer legally be kept as pets, but some species that originated in other countries are raised in captivity to provide companionship as well as entertainment. Some wild birds serve as game for licensed hunters. And wild birds provide endless enjoyment for bird-watchers and photographers. About 65 million Americans feed birds, spending about $2.5 billion every year on birdseed, feeders, and birdhouses, simply because they like to watch wild birds up close.

Our human fascination with birds has been the impetus for important inventions. Birds long stirred human yearnings for flight, leading to the design of modern airplanes. Hovering hummingbirds inspired the invention of the helicopter.

People not only marvel at the ability of birds to find their way home over great distances—we've exploited it for human communication. Ancient Romans caught and caged nesting swallows to send with athletes or spectators to distant sporting events. When a game was over, they tied a colored ribbon or yarn to the bird and released it. The swallow quickly returned to its mate and nest, where people, by seeing the ribbon color, learned the outcome of the game. Homing pigeons carried crucial military messages during World Wars I and II, and even today, the French military maintains pigeon corps to carry messages in the event that communications systems are damaged.

Birds also serve as valuable indicators of environmental quality. Their metabolic rate is faster than ours, and they are more sensitive to pollutants. Like the canaries whose deaths warned miners of poisonous gases, dying birds and diminishing bird populations warn of dangers that may be hurting us, too.

Birds are at the top of many food chains. Peregrine Falcons eat ducks and shorebirds that in turn eat fish, reptiles, amphibians, small aquatic invertebrates, and plants. Purple Martins and Common Nighthawks consume huge quantities of mosquitoes, mayflies, stoneflies, dragonflies, and other insects that live in water as eggs and nymphs. When any of these birds decline, we know something must be going wrong in our lakes and rivers. Common Redpolls eat birch seeds. When they decline, it may be because our northern forests are in trouble. Robins eat a great many earthworms in summer and may decline when pesticides such as malathion and diazinon in lawn sprays kill these worms (or even poison the robins outright). How can a lawn be healthy for people when the soil beneath it can't support worms? D.D.T.

**Working birds**
Some modern hospitals use homing pigeons to carry blood and tissue samples to laboratories— pigeons travel above heavy urban traffic without ever getting caught in gridlock or stopping at red lights.

**Flamingo facts**

People have decorated their lawns with wood and ceramic ornaments, including flamingos, for a long time, but the first plastic lawn flamingo was invented in 1957 by Don Featherstone at a Union Products company plant in Massachusetts. There are five species of real flamingos in the world—three from South America, one from Africa and India, and the Greater Flamingo, which is native to Europe, Africa, and Central and South America. This is the species that is most commonly found in zoos. The American race of this species very rarely wanders to south Florida. If flamingos don't eat enough shrimp, new feathers will be pale pink or white instead of deep pink.

was developed to kill insects, but until people started finding dead robins on their lawns, chemists and entomologists didn't realize that it also hurt mammals and birds. Learning about birds increases our understanding of the natural world and helps us figure out how to protect it.

Yes, birds are everywhere, touching and enriching every aspect of our lives. We adults may find deep satisfaction in developing our own awareness of birds. Although cursory background is all that's needed to introduce birds to kids, the more we learn, the richer the learning experiences we can provide children.

## A flurry of activities to get you started

Many fun activities can start children's creative juices flowing and get them thinking about birds and excited about studying them.

After explaining that different birds flap their wings in different ways, ask little kids to pretend that they are birds flapping their "wings." This activity can be instructive if you're teaching about hawk flight or wonderfully silly when somebody tries to be a hummingbird. Hawks riding on an updraft or thermal air current may soar, wings outstretched, without flapping for many minutes at a time. Eagles do this with their wings straight out, vulture wings held up in a shallow V, and Osprey with their wings bent slightly forward. (When little children draw letter M's in the sky to represent birds, they are unknowingly drawing Ospreys.) Hummingbirds flap their wings steadily at about sixty beats per second, chickadees at about twenty-seven beats per second, and crows at only two or three. Sharp-shinned Hawks usually flap rapidly a few times and then glide with their wings outstretched for a few seconds. Woodpeckers flap rapidly and then swoop with their wings closed for a second or two.

Using string, yarn, grasses, or similar materials, weave bird nests. Place the nests outside to determine whether they are as sturdy as those made by birds.

Create 3-dimensional birds using clay, cardboard, or

whatever other art media strike your fancy. One year, inspired by a university paper airplane contest, I assigned my seventh-graders a homework assignment to make a bird, real or imaginary, out of whatever materials they had on hand. On the day the assignment was due, our class was to go outside and have a contest seeing which bird flew farthest, but the kids made so many creative birds (some that they didn't want to endanger by tossing to the wind) that we ended up giving a wider variety of awards—for the bird that stayed aloft the longest, the one that flew the farthest (I believe the body of that one was a rock), the most realistic looking bird, the most fanciful, the silliest, the weirdest, etc.

Hold a wildlife art contest. One year I held one for grades six, seven, and eight. This activity was optional, not even for extra credit, and I was amazed at how many children entered. The quality of their work was breathtaking—as children saw the fine work of others, some took back their own entries to make improvements. I invited an editor of the local newspaper to serve as judge. He gave first, second, and third place awards and honorable mentions to all the work that he felt genuinely merited it. The children trusted his judgment since he obviously was impartial. He displayed all their artwork in the newspaper lobby for a few weeks, and then we displayed it in the school cafeteria for a month to inspire younger students.

Call children's attention to the birds in books. Fiction, such as *Owl Moon* by Jane Yolen, *Owls in the Family* by Farley Mowat, Jean Craighead George's wonderful books, or "Baker's Blue Jay Yarn," a short story by Mark Twain, can serve as springboards for bird study. Even books that aren't specifically about birds often mention them. In *White Fang*, Jack London talks of moose birds (these are really Gray Jays) and the ptarmigan chicks that became White Fang's first prey. In *The Long Winter*, Laura Ingalls Wilder's family discovers an oceanic bird (based on her description, probably a Dovekie or Ancient Murrelet) that was blown to their Dakota farm in a fierce storm. Integrating bird study into reading and language arts is especially rewarding

**Precious moments**

My most treasured bird artwork is a cardinal that was fashioned by my four-year-old son Joey entirely on his own. The body is a rock, with cardboard wings, tail, beak, and crest glued on, all painted with red and black tempera paints. What a wonderful Mother's Day surprise!

7

## Imaginary birds

Describe an imaginary habitat or a whole new planet and then ask the kids to each design a bird that could live there. If the atmosphere were less dense than earth's, birds might not need to be aerodynamically shaped. If the planet were entirely underwater, songbirds might have webbed feet. If the planet had longer nights than earth's, maybe birds would glow in the dark or have flashlight beam eyes—the whole point of this activity is for kids to let their imaginations run wild while still thinking critically.

## Silly bird pictures

Ask children to identify what's wrong with the birds on the next page.

All the diagrams and drawings in this book may be reproduced for educational purposes.

because it reinforces what is learned in both subjects and also broadens children's perspectives.

Have children write their own fiction, nonfiction, and poetry about birds, then collect it in a volume for a family or classroom library. Or collect comics with bird characters and display them on a bulletin board. Then ask kids to write and design their own four-panel comic strips with bird characters. Compile them into a classroom book. Some local Audubon chapter newsletters have (and all of them should have) a children's page on which some of the best work created by children is published. Look for contests and other opportunities for children's work to be recognized in the larger world.

Listen to bird song recordings and to live songs and calls outdoors. This activity can be jolly fun as well as instructive, and has a magical appeal to visually handicapped adults and children. I've had classes vote on the prettiest bird song, the most prehistoric-sounding, the loudest, the quietest, and the most insectlike. Every class I've ever taught voted the call of the Willow Ptarmigan (the state bird of Alaska) "The Official Weirdest Bird Call in the Universe." Once kids have heard a variety of calls, they may try doing imitations. Owl hoots and the whistled songs of White-throated Sparrows and various chickadees are the easiest, but some children can imitate much more difficult sounds. Junior high kids do especially well at loon calls. Bird-calling contests often work best when grown-ups are willing to abandon their own sense of dignity and join in the fun.

When we share our interest, curiosity, and love for birds with children in creative ways like this, we open their eyes and hearts to the wonder of birds all around us—birds real and imaginary, wild and domesticated, practical and whimsical, those that nourish our bodies and those that nourish our souls. Children's minds open like floodgates, allowing wave after wave of information to flow in. We adults are the engineers who help them manage that surging flow.

# WHAT IS WRONG WITH THESE PICTURES?

© Pfeifer-Hamilton Publishers • 210 West Michigan • Duluth, MN 55810        (218) 727-0500

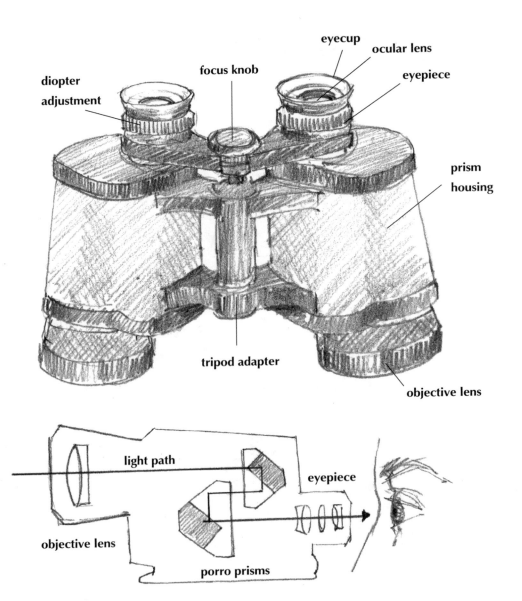

eyecup

ocular lens

eyepiece

diopter
adjustment

focus knob

prism
housing

tripod adapter

objective lens

light path

eyepiece

objective lens

porro prisms

# 2

# A FEW
# TOOLS OF
# THE TRADE

Simplify! Simplify! Thoreau's admonition would seem aptly applicable to bird study because birds are the ultimate light travelers. Thoreau watched them with no tools at all except his eyes, mind, heart, and a pencil and notebook, yet he wrote lovely things about them, noting that the junco is "leaden skies above, snow below," and "the bluebird carries the sky on his back."

Nature study in the nineteenth and early twentieth century required little more equipment than Thoreau's. Arm and Hammer put little bird cards, which bird fanciers collected and treasured, into boxes of baking soda at the turn of the twentieth century, but as we enter the twenty-first century, we have so many books, posters, audio and videotapes, computer programs, optical aids, and other resources available for teaching about birds that a comprehensive listing would be intimidating. When it comes right down to it, however, even in the computer age we can have avian encounters filled with joy, wonder, and learning using no more tools than Thoreau. When a pair of chickadees built a nest cavity in the box elder outside my bedroom window, I woke to their cheerful activities every morning for weeks, quickly recognizing the male by a few scraggly feathers on his face and the female by her unusually short tail. I gazed at them while lounging in bed, both unaided and unencumbered by binoculars. And

**Essential tools**

- curious mind
- watchful eyes
- listening ears

**Useful additions**

- pencil and notebook
- field guide
- binoculars

**Fun extras**

- other books
- audiotapes and CDs
- spotting scope
- bird calls
- owl decoys

my junior high classes had many rich bird experiences on nature hikes without binoculars or field guides. We must always be careful that the tools and equipment we use in bird study help, rather than hinder, our vision and enjoyment of birds. In this chapter, I list only the books, materials, and resources that I personally find indispensable.

## A guide to the field guides

Bird names aren't written in stone, but the American Ornithologists' Union has gone to a great deal of effort to ensure that the common names of birds are standardized. A "gopher" in Wisconsin is a different animal altogether from a "gopher" in the west, and what people in one place call a "lightning bug" is a "firefly" someplace else. But a Carolina Chickadee in South Carolina is the exact same species called a Carolina Chickadee everywhere else. Many birds also have nicknames—that same Carolina Chickadee is affectionately known as a "tomtit" in some places. Everyone is entitled to call birds whatever he or she wants—that which we call a Rose-throated Becard by any other name would sing as sweet. But for clear communication, we use field guides to identify and learn the standard names of birds. So the single most important bird book for children is a good field guide. The three best are: the Golden guide (*A Guide to Field Identification: Birds of North America*), the National Geographic guide (*Field Guide to the Birds of North America*), and Roger Tory Peterson's guide (*A Field Guide to the Birds East of the Rockies* or *A Field Guide to Western Birds*).

The Golden guide is attractive, the most compact, and the least expensive of the top three, and it includes every North American species. It has one unique feature—it provides *sonagrams* for most birds. Some people, including adults who are good at recognizing bird calls, can't figure out these graphic representations of sounds, but children and adults with a good ear for musical detail may find them enormously helpful. One minor drawback of the Golden guide: the softbound pages may eventually fall out. (Then again, that makes an old copy a great choice for making flashcards.) Also, the range maps are tiny, without state lines drawn in, so children and geographically impaired adults may have some trouble using them.

The National Geographic guide is considered by many advanced birders to be the best field guide available, but it's also the biggest—too hefty for little kids' hands, especially in the field. It includes every North American species. One silly note: try to get copies of both the first and second editions (first editions are in many libraries). Compare the drawings of the Connecticut Warbler in the two editions (page 370). Some readers had criticized the proportions of the feet in the first edition. The artist corrected the problem in the second edition by drawing leaves over the feet. Would this be an example of a cover-up or of turning over a new leaf? Kids will appreciate this graphic proof that grown-ups make mistakes.

Because the Peterson guide is available in eastern and western editions, it simplifies identification in some ways. For example, why should a Minnesota child be confronted with the twenty hummingbird choices shown in the Golden or National Geographic guides when the rubythroat is the only hummer normally found in the east? But pictures of the other choices do come in handy when a rarity shows up. Minnesota has several records of Rufous Hummingbirds, and on one or two occasions Anna's and Calliope Hummingbirds have also been recorded in the state. Older children—especially those whose interest has been ignited—usually prefer a field guide that shows every possibility, no matter how remote. If these children choose the Peterson guide, they'll probably want both editions. But plenty of other children prefer the Peterson guide precisely because it doesn't include every bird, leaving out choices which are genuinely impossible to find in a given area.

The Peterson guide has a unique and useful innovation—Roger Tory Peterson's distinctive arrows pointing to important

**Gift for a teacher**

A good field guide makes a thoughtful present for a family to give a favorite teacher at holiday time or at the end of the year. Both the teacher and future classes will benefit.

**Simple field guide**

To create a cheap and easy homemade field guide, make simple line drawings of the species most likely to be seen and photocopy them for every child.

field marks. This book also provides the most detailed and comprehensive range maps of any field guide, but these maps are so large that they are presented in a separate section in the back, too far from the pictures and species accounts to be convenient.

### Other field guides

Beginner field guides are designed especially for children, limiting their scope to the most common species. Small children will appreciate the bigger pictures and fewer choices in these books, which are attractive and often packed with interesting information. However, in my experience, older children will soon come across one of the hundreds of birds not shown in these simplified guides and feel frustrated that they can't find their bird in the book.

Photographic field guides simply aren't as good as field guides with paintings or drawings. Film type, lighting, and background affect colors, and sunlight or shadows may make a bird's colors appear washed out or very dark. The only available photograph of a particular species may show it at an angle that obscures an important field mark. Photographs limit your possibilities and generally allow only two or three species to be shown on a single page, making it necessary to thumb through many pages to narrow down a tricky identification. And because it's impossible to gauge distance in a photo, size comparisons between species are impossible to make.

Also, to keep them from being unwieldy for field use, photographic guides never include all the age and sex plumage variations within a species, and even the best new photographic guides leave out species that are relatively rare but occasionally seen at backyard feeders. No photographic guide includes pictures of ducks in flight or of their wing patterns, even though those are critical field marks. And photographic guides often select pictures of birds performing their most exciting displays, rather than in the poses we are more likely to see. A good artist can emphasize or minimize features that are more or less important for identification, make color differences clearer, and draw similar birds in the same pose to make comparisons easier. An artist can draw several different plumages side by side, include smaller drawings detailing characteristic wing patterns, behaviors, and displays and even add pictures of similar birds for comparison, all on a single page.

Some field guides arrange species by color, but this is impractical and even silly. Looking at an Eastern or Western Bluebird from the front on a cloudy day, we notice the reddish breast much more than the blue back, but we won't find the bird in the red section. A Bobolink is completely black from the front and white and yellow from behind—how can it be placed in a single color category? And the Painted Bunting is vivid red, blue, and green—hardly just one color. With this kind of organization, you practically need to know what the bird is in order to find it at all. The best field guides arrange birds *taxonomically*, the way ornithologists organize birds by their relationships to one another. As children use these guides, they eventually get better at figuring out where to find each bird in the book, and they learn a bit of taxonomy almost by osmosis.

Remember that a good field guide is supposed to be just that—an identification tool, accurate and complete yet small and handy for field use. For identification, choose the Golden, National Geographic, or Peterson guide, using other field guides and bird books as resources to enrich bird study beyond identification.

## How many field guides do you need?

If you're dealing with your own children or grandchildren, and if you can afford it, buy each child his or her own field guide. Many children are internally motivated to keep lists, taking deep satisfaction from checking off in their own personal field guide the birds they see. I gave each of my kids a

**Field guides**

- *A Guide to Field Identification: Birds of North America*, Second Edition, (nicknamed the Golden guide) by Chandler S. Robbins, Bertel Bruun, and Herbert S. Zim (Golden Press, New York, 1983)

- The National Geographic guide, *A Field Guide to the Birds of North America*, Second Edition (National Geographic Society, Washington, D.C., 1987)

- Roger Tory Peterson's *A Field Guide to the Birds East of the Rockies*, Fourth Edition (1980) and *A Field Guide to Western Birds*, Third Edition (1990) both published by Houghton Mifflin, Boston

**Teaching large groups of children**

Throughout this book, you'll find these little juncos and the words "especially for groups." That's your indication that the following material addresses the special needs of people working with groups of children.

National Geographic guide to commemorate the day their personal bird list reached fifty.

ESPECIALLY FOR GROUPS

Ideally all children should have their own field guide to use and take home for practicing identification independently. Having a few copies of other field guides may help with tricky identifications and may be useful for comparison.

Unfortunately, this isn't realistic in many schools. Some children may have field guides at home that they can bring to share, but others may have never even heard of them. One or two copies in the classroom are better than none, and resourceful teachers can set up learning centers where individual children work on identification activities while others are busy with other projects. At least one field guide should be available on all outdoor trips. If children are well prepared, it's possible they won't encounter unfamiliar birds on an outing, but rare and unusual birds do occasionally turn up even in the heart of large cities—for example, the first Snowy Owl I ever saw was flying right above Lake Shore Drive in downtown Chicago.

If only one or two field guides are available for a class bird trip, have the kids take turns looking up new birds or find them yourself and then pass the book around. At Hawk Ridge Nature Reserve in Duluth, Minnesota, I've seen resourceful teachers prepare large classes for hawk-watching trips using only one or two field guides.

**Other bird books**

In Appendix III, you will find a list of other excellent books on birds ranging from large reference books to inexpensive guides about ornithology, bird biology, conservation, and attracting birds. I have also listed some regional guides and children's books. I have described my personal favorites, but they are only a fraction of the thousands of books available in libraries and bookstores.

## Binocular basics

Although it's possible to provide quality birding experiences without binoculars, with them kids will obviously see many more birds and see them better. One of my birding buddies who sells optics told me that the whole point of binoculars is "to magnify the wonder of nature, not obscure it." Most of the best binoculars are made by companies that also make quality cameras or medical optics. The optics in cheaper brands may be poorly aligned, gather too little light, or have such generally poor quality that they could lead to eyestrain. If optics are poor, children get frustrated and may even be turned off to nature study altogether. There is no right answer to the question of which are the best binoculars to buy. You will take many different factors into account, beginning and ending with your budget.

Parents and grandparents can afford to use different criteria than school teachers or nature centers when selecting binoculars for kids. Even though binoculars are an invaluable tool for discovering and getting close to nature, I wouldn't buy a child a top-of-the-line, really expensive brand—either the child will be too conscientious, worrying so much about damaging a valuable pair that birding won't be fun, or the child won't be conscientious enough, and costly equipment will get broken. Stick to the low- or (preferably) mid-price range. The jump in quality between cheap and mid-range optics is much larger than the jump in quality between mid-range and top-line optics.

Every pair of binoculars is described by two numbers, such as 7x35 or 10x40. The first number is the *magnification power,* telling how much larger an object will appear. I recommend 7-power binoculars for beginners. These magnify the bird seven times and are strong enough for most needs. More powerful

**The invention of binoculars**
Hans Lippershey, a Dutch optician, invented the first telescope in 1608. A few months later, he got the idea of hooking up two telescopes side by side, inventing the first pair of binoculars. Modern binoculars have much lower magnification than telescopes, which are usually too bulky to fit side by side. People who see out of only one eye, who want very small field glasses for backpacking, or who want to save money sometimes use a monocular.

**Binoculars for kids**

- low- or mid-price range
- 7x35
- rubber armor
- interocular distance adjusts close
- long eye-relief
- sturdy eye cups

magnification will make the bird look bigger and closer, but at the expense of showing less background, making the bird harder to locate in the first place. Also, the stronger the binocular's power, the more the image will be distorted by shaking hands and heat shimmer. Don't increase the frustration level for beginners with binoculars that are too strong. You might even consider 6-power binoculars for small children.

The second number refers to the binocular's *aperture,* which is the diameter, in millimeters, of the big lens in the front of the binoculars (the *objective lens*). The bigger the aperture, the more light comes through, brightening the image, but also the heavier the binoculars are to lug around. A good rule of thumb is to choose binoculars with an aperture number at least five times the magnification number (i.e. 7x35, 8x40 or 10x50).

Wide-angle binoculars present a noticeably larger field than standard binoculars of the same magnification and lens size. This is a major advantage in situations like hawk-watching, where large streams of birds can be counted more accurately and appreciated more fully, but offsetting that advantage, the image through inexpensive wide-angle binoculars is sometimes fuzzy, with distorted edges. It can be hard to key in on a sitting bird against the bigger, busier background of wide-angle binoculars, but it's often easier to pick out flying birds through them.

I wouldn't even consider fixed-focus glasses, which can't focus at close range, or zoom binoculars, which are too heavy—both of these features also sacrifice way too much visual acuity to be worthwhile.

Rubber armor is a good idea, especially for binoculars used at nature centers or other facilities where groups of kids come and go so quickly that you don't have time to teach the fine points of binocular use and care. When you're selecting binoculars for children, try to bring along a real kid or two to check how comfortable the binoculars feel in their hands and on their necks. And make sure the interocular distance can be adjusted to accommodate the close-set eyes of young children.

## Matching eyes to optics

Most binoculars have helpful features that allow them to be tailored to a particular user's needs. *Eyecups* hold the *ocular lenses* (the lenses you actually look through) exactly the right distance from the eyes (this distance is called *eye relief)*, to optimize magnification and cut out peripheral light, making the image clearer and brighter. Eyecups should be extended if the user does not wear eyeglasses. Since eyeglasses hold binoculars away from the eyes and let in peripheral light anyway, eyecups should be retracted for eyeglass wearers. If you're buying binoculars specifically for a child who wears glasses, consider models with long eye relief (at least 15 mm). Unfortunately, binoculars with long eye relief are more expensive than comparable models without. All other things being equal, choose binoculars with eyecups that seem sturdy enough to withstand a lot of opening and closing, especially if several children will use them.

Virtually all binoculars on the market have *center focusing*, in which a single knob controls the focus for both eyepieces. People's eyes are seldom precisely matched, so to accommodate the visual difference between eyes, binoculars also have on one side or the other a *diopter adjustment* (a little knob numbered +2 to -2). To use binoculars without eyestrain, each user should adjust the knob to match the differences between his or her own eyes. The adjustment can be made in a large room as easily as outdoors. Give the children these directions:

1. Examine your binoculars. Find the center focus adjustment and the diopter adjustment.
2. Look at something a good distance away, like a picture, door knob, or swing set.
3. Keep both eyes open and use your hand to cover the

**Backwards binoculars**

While kids are practicing using their binoculars, someone will invariably hold them backwards to make everything look tiny. Explore this novel discovery. For a fun activity, look through binoculars backwards while holding a coin, pen, or other small item at arm's length. What will happen if you bring the item closer and closer to the binoculars? Kids are amazed to see binoculars transformed into crystal clear magnifying glasses. Once they learn this technique, they'll use binoculars to investigate the intricacies of all sorts of things, near and far.

lens on the side with the diopter adjustment. Use the center focus adjustment to focus the other side on your object.

4. Now switch hands, uncovering the lens with the diopter adjustment lens and covering the other lens. Focus again, but this time use the diopter adjustment.

5. Repeat the last two steps. The picture should be now perfectly focused for both eyes.

6. Look at the number setting on the diopter adjustment. It may be anywhere from +2 to -2. Memorize this setting—your eyes will always see best through this pair of binoculars when set on this number.

Occasionally remind kids to check their diopter adjustment setting. When children get new eyeglasses, they will probably need to figure it out all over again. Try to make sure children get the same pair of binoculars each time because there can be some differences among them. To keep track in a classroom, you can number them with an indelible marker. When children share binoculars with a partner, try to pair them by their diopter adjustment numbers and whether or not they wear eyeglasses so when they pass the binoculars back and forth they won't get a blurry image or have to waste time adjusting eyecups. Some married birders regret not checking out their partner's diopter adjustment number before making a lifetime commitment.

## Protecting optics

Before going outdoors with binoculars, shorten the neck straps to be just long enough to use comfortably. The longer the straps are, the more the binoculars will flop around, hitting belt buckles and bouncing on the ground when the kids lean over. If your child's binoculars come with loose lens caps, take them off ahead of time, or they will most assuredly get lost. When binoculars are stored in their cases or in a reasonably dust-free cabinet, lens caps aren't necessary anyway. Plastic rain guards fastened to the neck strap protect binoculars from rain and snow and also from sandwich crumbs and dripping juice. If the binoculars you choose don't come with these guards, you might ask a child to design some in an inventor's contest.

Teaching children respect and proper care for binoculars is easier when you're dealing with your own children or in teaching situations where children use the same binoculars for weeks or months rather than in groups that have only one or two short bird study sessions (such as at a nature center). You can show children how to clean the objective and ocular lenses (only when they're dirty!) by first brushing and blowing away any dust particles with a camera air brush and then wiping gently with a lint-free cloth. (Both inexpensive cleaning tools are available at camera stores.) Now and then clean rubber eyecups with a rubber conditioner (such as Armor All protectant, available at hardware stores). Never spray or pour liquids directly onto the eyecups—apply the protectant to a clean cloth.

## Looking good

Binoculars can be frustrating to use at first, and some children experience "image blackout" if their eyes aren't properly aligned with the lenses as they first look through them or if the interocular distance between the binocular's two telescopes is wider or narrower than the child's eyes. Encourage them to practice pushing or pulling the glasses together or apart to adjust this. Try to provide ample opportunities to practice looking at trees, signs, playground equipment, each other, and other things that hold relatively still before trying to watch unidentified flitting objects. To look at a distant object through binoculars, tell kids to keep their eyes on the object as they pull the binoculars up to their eyes. This trick takes a little time, but once they get the hang of it, it will quickly become second nature.

### Stars in their eyes

Bright binoculars (ones with a large objective lens) can provide excellent views of moon craters, the Orion nebula, and the moons of Jupiter.

Binoculars also make an exceptional viewing tool for solar eclipses. Don't look directly at the sun through them! Simply hold them in line with the sun, projecting the image of the eclipse onto a smooth surface (pavement or a piece of paper or cardboard on a lawn). The paired lenses of binoculars provide a double treat that a large group can see and enjoy together.

### A note about eyeglasses

School teachers don't have a say in the eyeglasses that students wear, but parents and grandparents do, and to protect little eyes for a lifetime of good vision, they should keep a few things in mind. Make sure every pair of eyeglasses has 100 percent UV protection for both UV-A and UV-B wavelengths. In bright sun, it's much safer to wear regular eyeglasses with UV protection than sunglasses without it because sunglasses reduce brightness, causing pupils to dilate and actually allowing more UV light into the eyes. Experienced bird-watchers generally don't wear sunglasses or tinted eyeglasses because they distort color too much. A wide-brimmed hat protects both eyes and skin from dangerous UV light, but good luck getting a kid to wear one. Remind them that baseball cap brims are designed to protect their eyes, not the back of their neck.

The closer to the eyes that eyeglasses sit, the larger the image we see through binoculars. When I switched from a pair of glasses with thick frames to thinner frames that sat closer to my eyes, it was as if I had bought a brand-new, more powerful pair of binoculars, too. If you buy your child eyeglasses with plastic lenses, make sure they're guaranteed against scratching. Even so, they may slowly develop circular scratches from the binoculars. To minimize this, keep binocular eyecups clean and always replace broken or missing eyecups before use.

### Spotting scopes

If you're birding with children, a spotting scope on a tripod can be a wonderful aid. Although most birders use scopes mainly for waterfowl and shorebirds that don't flit around much, they also provide fine looks at cooperative songbirds and are especially great insurance that everyone is seeing the same bird. Teachers without spotting scopes might ask their local Audubon chapter to mention in their newsletter that the school needs one. More than one birder with an expensive new scope is likely to have an old one sitting in a closet. If you're planning to look at songbirds as well as more distant water birds, it's probably best, if you have a choice, to use a fixed 20-power eyepiece. Spotting scopes also work well for looking at the moon, planets, and stars.

## Bird recordings

A wide variety of bird recordings are on the market: virtually all on cassette, many on CD, and some still available on vinyl records.

Most people tune out after listening to a dozen or so bird songs, and hardly anyone wants to learn bird songs in the order they're placed on a recording, so I strongly advise against purchasing prerecorded cassettes. To find given songs or calls on cassettes, you have to keep fast-forwarding and reversing, an annoying process that eventually stretches and ruins the tape. Cassette tapes may also get unwound, especially when little kids use them.

CDs produce the finest sound quality. Some of the older ones were recorded with several species on each "track," but many now include only one species per track, allowing fast and easy "cuing up" of bird songs.

If you have access to both a CD player and a cassette recorder, the best solution is to dub a few selected songs from the CD to a blank tape. This is considered fair use as long as you own the CD or, in the case of a library loan, as long as you erase the cassette when you return the CD. As children master one group of songs, you can simply tape a new batch. This system works for records, too, and is a great technique for adults as well as kids to study bird songs. If you want to quiz kids on bird calls, tape the songs from a CD, leaving out the narration.

I use bird recordings in many teaching situations for kindergartners, Elderhostelers, and everyone in between. The most comprehensive single sets are: the Cornell Laboratory of

Ornithology's *Peterson Field Guides: Eastern/Central Bird Songs* (1990), which includes over 250 species, and *Peterson Field Guides: Western Bird Songs* (1991), including songs of 522 species. (Both are published by Houghton Mifflin Company, Boston.) These sets are available both on CD and cassette tape. The selections are short but include the most typical vocalizations. The eastern edition inexplicably leaves out the introduced House Sparrow, European Starling, and Rock Dove (common pigeon) despite the fact that these are the most common birds near most schools, but the western edition includes them. Both editions leave out songs of endangered birds, presumably to keep birders from stressing vulnerable birds by playing recordings in the field to attract them. The western edition includes the call of the Willow Ptarmigan, which every one of my classes has voted the "Official Weirdest Bird Call in the Universe." The narrator cites the name of each species before the call is played.

Lang Elliott's A *Guide to Night Sounds, Wild Sounds of the Northwoods*, and *Know Your Bird Sounds—Volumes One* and *Two* (NorthWord Press, Minocqua, Wisconsin, 1994) are inexpensive and available on both CD and tape. These sets include fewer species than the Peterson recordings, but each species is covered far more completely. The robin selection on *Know Your Bird Sounds*, for example, includes the typical song, a special continuous song variation, and five different calls, along with comments by the narrator that are brief, to-the-point, and helpful in explaining what each different call means. A *Guide to Night Sounds* and *Wild Sounds of the Northwoods* provide mammal, amphibian, and insect calls in addition to bird songs, and although these recordings don't identify the context of the vocalization on the actual recording, an accompanying booklet for each set provides plenty of information.

When I was a neophyte birder, a whistled song kept me searching every evening for weeks before I discovered that my "bird" was really a little frog called a spring peeper. I sort of wish I'd had one of Lang Elliott's recordings back then to help me figure our nonavian calls, but come to think of it, I had lots of fun tramping through the wet swamp in search of the singer. I'll never forget the thrill of finally finding that one-inch-long little songster clinging to a leaf in the dusk.

**Peculiar devices**

The Audubon Bird Call is a little wood-and-metal contraption. When you rub the wood around the metal, it produces various chirps and squeaks. Sleeping owls and students perk right up when you play with one of these, and kids love to see how many sounds they can make with them. My bird caller can make a pretty accurate cardinal call when I work it right. I used it a lot on walks with my Brownie and Girl Scout troop, squeaking it as a signal that it was time to pay attention. It's quiet enough that kids often keep their voices down on their own so they'll notice when it's played.

Hawks and falcons are quite helpless in the dark, and owls like to eat them, so by day, whenever hawks spy an owl, they try to drive it away. If you live on a migration flyway, a plastic owl decoy is a great device for enticing hawks down from above during migration. If you tape a few real feathers to it, the slight movement should be enough to make any stranger in the neighborhood take a second or even a third look. Merlins and Sharp-shinned Hawks sometimes fly at an owl decoy half a dozen times or more—I think when they realize it's a fake they get angrier at it for tricking them. Plastic owls make a great family or classroom mascot when they're not working. They're available at hardware and outdoor stores.

A simple hand mirror can serve as a fine pointer. With practice, you can direct reflected sunlight from the mirror to where you want kids to look. Never point a light beam directly at a bird—it's downright rude, plus it will make the bird fly away. Rather, move the beam in a circular pattern around

**Good reflections**

Tie a small hand mirror to a stick or yardstick to see a reflection of the eggs or baby birds in a high nest without climbing the tree or scaring the birds too much. You can even use an inexpensive hand mirror to illuminate and reflect the contents of burrows and holes in the ground, enabling you to peek at snakes, mammals, and burrowing owls.

**Birding the net**

The Internet includes many bird-related sites, providing photos, educational material, birding hotlines, migration data, and interesting bird banter from all over. Internet resources are in such a state of flux that specific recommendations are not possible, but most web-browsing software will furnish access to a variety of sites. The Cornell Laboratory of Ornithology's education department provides education information over the net and links to selected sites and should be a continuing reliable source for web browsers. The Lab's World-Wide Web address is http://www.ornith. cornell.edu/.

the bird or right below it. Don't get too dependent on the mirror; eventually the sun will go behind a mass of clouds or will be behind you in the sky when the bird is in front, and you won't be able to point its reflection in the right direction.

If you're rich, shine the red beam of a laser pointer or gun sight around birds to point them out on cloudy days. If you know a hunter who will lend you one, it may be a great help when a rare warbler flits in and you want everyone to see it before it flits away. Never allow children to play with lasers—they can cause serious burns or damage retinas.

**Videos and computer software**

I strongly recommend against using videos or movies about natural history with children except for specific, special purposes, such as teaching about the mechanisms of flight. My own father-in-law once asked me why I spend so much time searching for birds outside when I could see them a lot closer and easier just watching nature shows. Like him, kids may become impatient with the natural world after seeing these programs. Children have little understanding of the long hours and hard work involved in filming wildlife—after they've seen video footage of birds, they sometimes seem disappointed that real birds don't come closer. Give them the opportunity to see, hear, smell, and touch the real natural world rather than to merely watch it vicariously.

Computer software designed to teach about birds may also serve to make kids impatient with the natural world. Some programs are gimmicky without any meat, providing less information than a simple book. The best programs include a wealth of information and sometimes recordings and film footage, but again, learning from good books is more consistent with the natural rhythms of birds. On the other hand, programs designed to help maintain bird lists can be an excellent introduction to databases and spreadsheets.

## Resources for bird study

Many companies and institutions sell items useful for bird study. Three nonprofit organizations offer just about everything a grown-up could want for teaching kids about birds: the Cornell Laboratory of Ornithology, the American Birding Association, and the National Geographic Society.

The Cornell Laboratory, a division of Cornell University, is a nonprofit membership organization for the study, appreciation, and conservation of birds. Members receive the Lab's magazine, *The Living Bird Quarterly*, and its quarterly newsletter, *Birdscope*. You don't need to be a member to order materials from the Crow's Nest Birding Shop, which offers an enormous array of books, recordings, posters, binoculars, and field equipment. The Lab also offers photographic slides of just about every North American bird.

The Lab is committed to developing educational programs that dovetail with avian research and conservation. For many years they've administered Project FeederWatch, in which volunteers throughout the continent keep track of birds at their feeders. Data collected by these volunteers is processed at the Lab, providing valuable information about bird populations continent-wide. The Lab has also developed an offshoot of the project specifically for upper elementary and middle school classes. The nominal fee for participating covers the cost of printing and mailing materials—you do not need to be a member of the Lab to participate.

The Lab also offers Project PigeonWatch, designed to give urban as well as suburban and rural children opportunities to study nature and make genuine contributions to ornithological research. This project helps children build their powers of observation, learn careful note-taking, practice math and writing skills, and learn about the process of science. Research activities for children include documenting the different feather colors in a flock, observing courtship

**General resources**

The Cornell Laboratory of Ornithology
159 Sapsucker Woods Road
Ithaca, NY 14850
607-254-BIRD

The American Birding Association
P. O. Box 6599
Colorado Springs, CO 80904
1-800-634-7736.

National Geographic Society
1145 17th Street N.W.
Washington, D C. 20036
1-800-NGS-LINE.

behaviors, and conducting feeding experiments. Again, the nominal participation fee is well worth it.

For adults, the Lab also offers correspondence courses in ornithology and field courses in recording bird sounds.

Write to the Lab for further information about Lab programs or to get a copy of the Crow's Nest catalog.

The American Birding Association is a nonprofit membership organization whose mission is to promote recreational birding, contribute to the development of bird identification and population study, and help foster public appreciation of birds and their vital role in the environment. Members receive the bimonthly magazine, *Birding,* and the monthly newsletter *Winging It.* A. B.A. also publishes a youth newsletter, *A Bird's-Eye View,* produced by and for teenagers.

A. B.A. focuses on the sport of birding, emphasizing bird-finding and identification over biology and behavior, and so their sales department offers materials not available through the Cornell Lab. For example, people who wish to learn which birds live in their area or state can get a regional birder's guide or checklist from A.B.A. Sales. The American Birding Association also publishes birding hotline telephone numbers from all over the country—if your area has a hotline, it may be an essential source of information about the best places to find a wealth of birds as well as locations where you may find rarities. If your children have a foreign pen pal or are simply curious, you can even get field guides and recordings covering the birds of other countries. A.B.A. Sales also offers binoculars, spotting scopes, and field equipment. You don't need to be a member to order any of these materials.

Write to A.B.A. for information about the organization or to A.B.A. Sales for a catalog.

The National Geographic Society focuses on geography rather than ornithology, but it produces several excellent bird books, including a colorful and authoritative coffee table book and the finest field guide available. The monthly magazine for members often has fascinating, authoritative articles about birds. It also publishes a wonderful line of pop-up books in a series called "National Geographic Action Books," some of which are about birds. These are not run-of-the mill pop-up books for tiny tots—the artwork is beautiful, the paper engineering wonderfully creative and complicated, and the information fascinating, even for adults. National Geographic also offers a wonderful, inexpensive map of bird migration covering North and South America. Write to the National Geographic Society for more information.

## Sources for bird biology projects

To study bird anatomy and biology, it's helpful to get preserved pigeons and sparrows, lab manuals for pigeon dissection, owl pellet kits, and dissection tools and equipment. If you want the inside scoop on birds, these items are available from various commercial biological supply houses. Many of these companies sell only to educational institutions, but NASCO also sells to private individuals.

Mealworms can be useful for certain pet birds and for feeding wild birds. Chickadees often learn to take mealworms right from children's hands. You can get mealworms in small quantities at many pet shops, but if you wish to raise them for feeding birds, you might want to order 500 or 1000 to start with. They cost about $5 per thousand plus shipping and handling. Mealworms can be purchased from Grubco Inc. or from Rainbow Mealworms. Mealworms are easy to keep alive: just fill a plastic bucket or other tall container with a few inches of oatmeal, and now and again add a cut-up carrot or potato to provide moisture and additional nutrients. I raise mealworms at home, and whenever I peel carrots or potatoes, I put the peelings in my mealworm buckets. Even when mealworms reach adulthood (they turn into black beetles), they can't get out of an open ice cream bucket unless you knock it over.

**Bird biology resources**

NASCO
901 Janesville Avenue
Fort Atkinson, WI 53538
414-563-2446
FAX 414-563-8296

NASCO
4825 Stoddard Road
Modesto, CA 95356-9318
209-545-1600
FAX 209-545-1669.

Grubco Inc.
Box 15001
Hamilton, OH 45015
1-800-222-3563 .

Rainbow Mealworms
Box 4907
Compton, CA 90224
1-800-777-WORM.

# 3

## Attracting BIRDS to HOME and SCHOOL

All of us enjoy observing birds at close range from the comfort of indoors. There are many ways of enticing wild birds to feed and even nest nearby so children can study and enjoy them up close and personal. Bird feeders attract a wide variety of seed-eating and insectivorous birds, along with an occasional carnivore—a hawk, owl, or shrike attracted by the activity and hoping to catch a bird or mouse. The number of birds that will visit a feeding station depends entirely on the quality of the habitat and the types of food offered.

Pet birds, although neither wild nor native to America, can also be a rich resource for bird study and enjoyment, providing lessons in avian behavior and learning capacity, serving as models for artwork and distractions at homework time, and giving children something to love and care for. They are a welcome addition to many homes and classrooms.

### Bird feeders
More bird species can be attracted to feeders than most people realize. The more kinds of food you offer, the more birds you will entice. Woodworking projects to build feeders are fun to do with children. Plans for one feeder are included in Appendix II.

**Feeder housekeeping**
Whether at home or at
school, make sure to keep
feeders clean and the
ground beneath them raked
to prevent the spread of
avian diseases like botulism
and aspergillosis. And make
sure feeders are well
drained so seed doesn't
spoil. It is the height of
rudeness to invite birds to
dine just to send them off
with food poisoning.

Appendix III lists resources for building and maintaining bird
feeders, and your library may have more.

Teachers wishing to set out feeders are sometimes ham-
pered by school policy. Some districts don't allow seed storage on site for fear of attracting mice or rats. Some grounds
keepers and maintenance personnel won't mow around feeders set on poles or dislike piles of empty shells on the ground.
Teachers can get around some rules by storing seed at home
and bringing in a bucketful at a time, suspending hanging
feeders from trees and swing sets, or sticking acrylic feeders
with suction cups to windows. Sunflower hearts eliminate
messy shell residues—they're more expensive than whole sunflower seeds, but at least you're paying only for edible parts.
If you can't maintain a feeding station throughout the year,
you might at least scatter mixed seed on the ground during
spring and fall migration to see if juncoes and sparrows discover it, or hang oranges and nectar feeders up in May—
oriole and hummingbird migrants may notice the bright
colors as they wing overhead.

**Birdseed**
When most people think of feeders, they think of birdseed.
One of the easiest ways to attract a variety of birds year-round
is with sunflower seed. To make a simple sunflower seed feeder,
cut a big hole in the side of a clean bleach bottle, poke two or
three tiny holes in the bottom for drainage, tie twine or wire
around the handle to hang it from a tree limb or swing set,
and fill the bottom with sunflower seeds. Slicing through heavy
plastic with sharp scissors requires strength and care, so this
project isn't recommended for small children. Chickadees like
these hanging feeders, but so do squirrels—when they chew a
hole big enough that the seeds fall out, it's time to recycle that
feeder and make a new one. Glass mason jars or peanut butter
jars make unchewable feeders, but you'll end up with broken
glass if squirrels chew through string or rope, so hang these

feeders with wire only. Stores that sell bird feed also sell inexpensive gadgets that transform pop bottles into feeders.

Some birds prefer open platforms. A small piece of plywood set on a garbage can or barrel makes a fine dining table for grosbeaks, finches, and others. In Appendix II, you'll find a plan for a small platform feeder.

Mixed seed (the kind available in grocery stores) and cracked corn may attract doves and sparrows. Juncoes and other native sparrows also find white millet attractive. These ground feeders come most readily to low platform feeders or seeds scattered on the ground.

Niger seed appeals to redpolls, siskins, and goldfinches. Niger is also called thistle seed, but it's imported from India and is only distantly related to our native weed. Since the United States Department of Agriculture requires niger seed to be sterilized, it won't germinate on your lawn anyway. Because this seed is long and thin, offer it in a special niger seed feeder, which has the added benefit of giving small finches their own private feeder where larger birds can't compete. Some of these feeders are very inexpensive—unfortunately, the niger seed itself can cost more per pound than T-bone steak.

## Suet

Many seed-eating birds also need animal fat and protein which they obtain from insects, animal carcasses, and suet. Raw suet is simply fat trimmings—that sold in stores generally comes from beef. *Rendered suet* has been cooked and strained. Grocery stores used to give suet away but now usually charge for it. Stores that sell bird feed also sell suet cakes, which are made of rendered suet mixed with other ingredients like peanuts or even insect parts. Rendering your suet or melting it to make suet cakes is a job for a grown-up or for a child under close supervision. Melted fat reaches dangerously high temperatures and can cause serious burns. Raw suet is a bit more nourishing than rendered, but it gets rancid quickly

**Chickadees at lunch**
Many small birds will eat seeds placed in a shallow bowl or on a platform.

**How many sunflower seeds are in a fifty-pound bag of seeds?**

When Joey was six years old, he asked this question, so we figured it out as a family. We weighed out five ounces of seeds and counted them one by one—almost exactly 3,000. That meant there were about 9,600 per pound, or 480,000 per bag—almost half a million.

when the temperature rises above freezing. Rendered suet keeps surprisingly well even in summer.

Scrape suet onto pine cones and attach them to tree branches, or offer it in onion bags, in feeders made of hardware cloth, or in store-bought plastic-coated suet feeders. Suet may attract chickadees, nuthatches, woodpeckers, jays, and, unfortunately, starlings. Some commercially-sold suet feeders are designed to discourage starlings.

**Peanut butter**

Peanut butter is even more attractive than suet for some birds, and is safer for small children to mix with seeds. Pine cones make fine peanut butter feeders, or drill inch-wide holes into a piece of branch two to three inches in diameter to hold peanut butter globs. (These feeders are good for serving rendered suet, too.) Some people stick dowel perches beneath each hole, but most birds attracted to peanut butter and suet are perfectly capable of clinging to branches without a perch. Some people mix peanut butter with corn meal to prevent it from sticking to birds' mouths when it gets goopy and soft in warm weather.

**Getting out the word**

A feeding station may offer a wide variety of quality fare and still be worthless if birds don't come to it. Sometimes birds simply don't notice feeders at first. A tiny acrylic feeder stuck on a window may never attract the attention of a single bird, especially if the habitat is poor or the area is noisy. Scatter a handful of seeds on a window ledge or on the ground beneath an acrylic feeder to make it more noticeable. In an apartment or school setting, you might set feeders along the edge of a parking lot or in another relatively quiet spot within view of your windows. Begin feeding during late summer and fall or in spring, when birds are most likely to be exploring your area.

ESPECIALLY FOR GROUPS

Teachers are most likely to be successful at attracting birds when they start feeding during summer vacation, when birds aren't frightened from schools and playgrounds by the noise and bustle of playing children. Once they discover the feeders, they'll probably continue to visit them even with children about. If your setting simply doesn't harbor many birds, try to improve the habitat with plantings. Teachers may find a sympathetic nearby homeowner who would allow classes to visit the yard occasionally. A common interest in birds can draw odd assortments of people together.

---

### Nuts to you

Chickadees, nuthatches, jays, and squirrels prefer peanuts over just about anything. Set out a handful of whole, roasted peanuts on a windowsill or deck railing—it's fun watching squirrels and jays race to see which can grab the most in the shortest time. Blue Jays often hold and weigh each seed in their beaks before carrying off the heaviest one.

Chickadees and nuthatches seldom fly off with a whole peanut (though I once watched a Black-capped Chickadee lug a triple-seed peanut across my yard to a lilac bush, where it spent two hours stuffing itself). Peanut chips or hearts placed in a plastic mesh onion bag will make these little birds happy—at least until squirrels discover it.

I buy unsalted nuts when they're available, but don't worry if the only ones a store has in stock are salted. Birds, especially winter finches, are attracted to salt because their body gets depleted of minerals. If given in moderation, a bit of salt won't hurt them. Do make sure the peanuts have been roasted. Raw peanuts contain a chemical called a trypsin inhibitor that interferes with the absorption of protein.

Squirrels, jays, and chickadees also love walnuts and other

### Fun with seed feeders

Set a straw hat or a scarecrow dressed in gloves and wide-brimmed hat on a lawn chair, picnic table, or platform near a feeding station. Keep the hat brim and glove palms filled with seeds. After a week or two, when birds are coming regularly, sneak out, put the hat and gloves on, and stand in the same spot holding very still. Birds may alight on you. This is fun no matter how old you are. Many quiet, patient children have trained their backyard birds to take seeds right from their hands.

nuts—crack the hardest nuts open before setting them on a platform feeder. Some grown-ups don't like squirrels, but try explaining why to a three-year-old! Squirrels will go to amazing lengths to get nuts. Older children (and adults) delight in designing complicated puzzles that the squirrels must figure out in order to get a peanut or walnut.

Children are so drawn to squirrels and chipmunks that they may wish to train them to feed from their hands. But even the nicest, cutest squirrels and chipmunks may be highstrung or nervous and may bite even the most careful, mature child. Because of the remote but real possibility that any wild mammal can carry rabies, any animal that has bitten a person needs to be examined by a veterinarian. In the case of squirrels and other wild critters, that examination usually requires the animal to be euthanized—any child would feel horribly responsible if this happened. And when a squirrel or chipmunk has been "trained" to take peanuts from one person, it may expect others to treat it, too, approaching children who may be terrified of rodents. So classes and nature center visitors should never be allowed to entice these endearing creatures to approach too close.

As a wildlife rehabilitator, I raised a baby gray squirrel with help from my children. We released her in our yard, and even as she became completely independent, she continued to visit us for companionship and special treats. After three years, Chuckie still comes to our hands and is so gentle and reliable that I allow my kids to feed and hold her. They also feed certain other neighborhood squirrels that I have come to trust but may offer only the biggest peanuts, extended out far from their fingertips. Parents and grandparents use their own good judgment in this matter—teachers and naturalists should err on the side of caution.

### For a sweet tooth—er, beak

Hummingbirds and orioles that sip nectar from flowers often

are attracted to sugar water. Use one quarter cup of sugar per cup of water. Even though birds prefer it sweeter, never make a sugar-water mixture stronger than that because, without enough fresh water to metabolize the sugar, they may become dehydrated. Never substitute honey even though it seems so much more natural and nutritious than processed sugar. A fungus that grows on honey doesn't affect humans at all but may cause a mouth and tongue disease in birds.

Red food coloring is not only unnecessary in sugar water, it's actually harmful. Some long-term studies on captive hummingbirds connect food dyes with cancer and other diseases. Hummingbirds are attracted to the color red, but virtually every hummingbird feeder has red parts conspicuous enough to attract these keen-eyed little birds.

Change the water and clean hummingbird feeders every day or two. Sugar water ferments, and the process speeds up so much in warm weather that two-day-old sugar water may begin to cause liver damage. If the water becomes cloudy or if a dark fungus forms, wash and boil the feeder, or clean it with bleach or salt water and rinse and dry it thoroughly.

Hummingbird feeders may or may not have perches. Like humans, most hummers seem to prefer sitting down to dinner, but they clearly don't object to hovering at feeders. Oriole feeders look like oversized hummingbird feeders with large perches. Orioles and hummingbirds also feed at bowls of sugar water, as may migrating warblers. Use a red or orange plastic bowl to get them to notice it.

If bees or wasps become a problem, rub a little insect repellant on the feeder ports. Of course, if you have children with allergies to bees, don't risk using sugar-water feeders at all.

During spring migration, orioles often come to chunks of oranges. Cut an orange in half and tie the halves to a tree (branches are still bare when most orioles return) or set them on a platform feeder or window ledge. You can make an orange feeder from a five- by seven-inch piece of wood. Drill a

**Fruit flies for hummingbirds**
To improve the chances of attracting and keeping hummers, you might try putting melon or banana chunks in a mesh bag near your hummingbird feeder. This will attract fruit flies which provide necessary protein for hummingbirds. Children and grown-ups will enjoy the tiny hummers zipping this way and that, chasing almost-invisible flying insects.

**Photo fun!**
If you have a long cable release for your camera, set the camera on a tripod or stepladder close to a hummingbird feeder to give a child a wonderful first experience with bird photography. The child should hide as far away from the feeder as the cable release allows and when a hummer zips in, click!

hole in the center, push a four- to five-inch-long dowel through, and impale orange halves on the dowel ends.

Orioles seldom eat oranges after migration ends, at least in the upper Midwest, but throughout the summer they often come to sugar-water feeders and to grape jelly spooned into plastic bowls. Catbirds, thrashers, and some warblers are also fond of grape jelly. When my daughter, Katie, was three, she liked eating jelly-bread sandwiches at our picnic table while a catbird ate jelly from a bowl right next to her.

## Fun with hummingbirds

In areas where hummingbirds are abundant, they often get so tame (or so greedy) that they'll come to a feeder even while a person is carrying it. At one hummingbird feeding station in the southwest, visitors are sometimes given sugar-water feeders to hold out. Not only do hummingbirds come right to their hands to feed, one optimistic or confused little hummer actually stuck its tongue into a gentleman's ear!

## Other items to offer birds

Some people set out bread or donuts for birds. Unless the weather has been severe, I never do this during summer or winter, in part because these items aren't nutritious enough for seedeaters and in part because they attract too many House Sparrows, starlings, and pigeons. But during April and May migration, these items sometimes attract warblers and tanagers to platform feeders.

Jays, crows, and ravens like both dry and canned dog food, which are very nutritious for them. Unfortunately, these crow relatives, or *corvids*, are flourishing at the expense of other species because during nesting season they feed their own babies the eggs and nestlings of other birds. Even though I have an enormous soft spot for the crow family, I figure they probably don't need any extra subsidies from humans, but I must admit that I sometimes take pity and set out a few chunks of dog food for them when the temperature drops to twenty or thirty below zero.

Many of the beautiful birds that winter in the tropics eat insects. Flycatchers may come to fruit flies at mesh bags filled with chunks of melon or banana. A wide variety of birds, from bluebirds and tanagers to warblers, will devour mealworms. Chickadees, wrens, and bluebirds may even alight on a hand once they figure out where the mealworms are coming from. Sources of mail order mealworms are included in Chapter 2.

Egg shells provide calcium, which is especially important during nesting season when female birds may become calcium-depleted. Scatter crushed shells on a platform feeder along with seeds.

Some winter finches eat conifer and birch seeds almost exclusively and, because of their limited diet, may suffer minor mineral deficiencies. They also need grit in their gizzards to help with digestion. To get grit and minerals at once, they sometimes scrape tiny bits of mortar from chimneys and brick buildings. They're also fond of salt and grit on winter roads, but this can be a fatal attraction. Far safer are children's sandboxes. Our family sandbox has lured in White-winged and Red Crossbills, Pine and Evening Grosbeaks, redpolls, siskins and Purple Finches—sometimes while my kids were still playing in it! One of my favorite sandbox memories is of a glowing red Pine Grosbeak perched atop a bright yellow Tonka truck as three-year-old Tommy pushed another truck all around, making zooming noises. Tommy wore a yellow hard hat on top of his winter cap, and the grosbeak studied him almost as if wondering where it could get a tiny hard hat for itself.

## Bird baths

Bird baths provide drinking water as well as a place for birds to bathe. In areas where rainfall is plentiful, bird baths are most heavily used during droughts and in winter, but in arid regions where birds receive barely enough water for survival, bird baths may serve a critical function year-round. You can buy a terra cotta or stone bird bath, build a recirculating waterfall, or simply set a bowl of water on a platform feeder or wide porch railing.

The sound of dripping or running water attracts a wide variety of thirsty birds including wrens, thrushes, warblers, tanagers, and other species that can't be attracted to feeders. Try suspending a jug of water with a slow leak to make enticing dripping sounds. One of my Montana birding buddies once ran a hose on the ground to water a newly-planted tree. The water hit a piece of bark just right, making a little splashing fountain about five inches high. Every one of the thirty or so siskins and finches that had been drinking fresh water from his bird bath suddenly zipped to the splashing water, abandoning the bath. As long as the hose was on, producing that magnetic splashing and dripping, not one bird would drink from the ordinary birdbath.

During winter, when natural water is frozen, I sometimes set out a plastic bowl of water first thing in the morning and bring it in when ice forms. I don't use a heater. On the coldest days, even without a heater the water forms steam that can penetrate and coat feathers, reducing their insulation value. If the temperature is too mild for steaming, the water stays liquid long enough to satisfy my neighborhood birds' thirst. Many people do have great success with bird bath heaters. They are probably safe for birds except during severe cold.

## Birdhouses and nest materials

Nest boxes may attract cavity nesters from wrens and bluebirds to screech owls and some ducks, or they may sit empty for years, all depending on your habitat. There are many excellent books with construction plans and information about how to successfully attract birds to birdhouses—see Appendix III.

Whether or not your yard is appropriate for nest boxes,

providing materials for lining nests will attract many birds. Some of the most eagerly sought nest materials include feathers, dog fur (save it after brushing), clumps of cotton quilt batting or cotton balls (teased apart to loosen the fibers), and four- to six-inch lengths of unraveled binder twine or cotton string. Set nesting materials in mesh bags or clean suet feeders, or just stick them in a tree crevice, and watch the birds come!

Never offer birds dryer lint. Nice fluffy lint straight from the clothes dryer feels perfect to both us and birds. But when dryer lint gets wet, it draws together, shrinking and stiffening. If incorporated into a nest, lint may cause the whole structure to disintegrate after the first rain.

Don't offer white or colorful yarns. Ornithologists used to set out bright colors to make nest-finding easier, but this also helps predators in search of scrambled eggs for breakfast. Only offer yarn or string pieces that are shorter than four to six inches to protect baby birds and even adults from strangling.

## Fun with nesting materials

Tree Swallows line their nests with white feathers. The number of baby swallows that successfully fledge correlates with the number of white feathers in the nest, which insulate the babies against both excessive heat and cold. During early spring, as you walk along any beach, collect gull feathers—especially small body feathers. When swallows are flying about near nest boxes, toss some of these feathers to the wind. As soon as the swallows figure out what's happening, they'll mill about you, and some may daintily snatch feathers right from your hands.

## Plants that attract birds

Many excellent books and pamphlets explain how to attract wildlife with plantings. Because climate and soil conditions vary from place to place, find local resources who can give you specific plant recommendations. Agricultural extension offices,

**Provide safe homes**

Dense shrubbery provides hiding places from predators. Arbor vitae makes an especially good shelter for early spring nesting and safe sleeping year-round.

university horticulture departments, local bird clubs, and gardening stores can all be of help. A few general principles apply everywhere.

Birds depend on habitat for food, shelter, and protection from predators. Trees and shrubs that produce berries, such as dogwoods, elderberry, honeysuckle, juneberry, mountain ash and serviceberry, provide food during late summer, migration and winter. Robins and waxwings are especially attracted to winter berries. Buckthorn and highbush cranberry fruits taste bitter enough that birds seldom eat them when they first ripen, but by the end of winter, when other food sources are depleted, these berries become an important food source.

Cherry and crab-apple trees provide not only fruit but also nectar and blossoms. In spring, hummingbirds sip sweet liquid as Cedar Waxwings eat the petals. The many insects attracted to the flowers feed a variety of warblers, vireos, and other spring migrants that pass through during apple blossom time.

Orioles nest in elms. Evening Grosbeaks are attracted to box elder seeds. Birches, which hold their seeds through the winter, provide a major food source for redpolls. In years when cones are abundant, spruce and pine trees attract many winter finches. The first migrants to return to my yard each spring—Yellow-bellied Sapsuckers, Ruby-crowned Kinglets, and Yellow-rumped Warblers—come to my aspen tree for insects attracted to newly-opened catkins. The first hummingbirds to arrive feed at sapsucker drill holes in the same tree. Willows attract insects and the birds that eat them.

Many flowers attract hummingbirds, especially red flowers with "throats." Fuschias, petunias, delphiniums, larkspur, coral bells, jewelweed, viburnum, and verbena are all good choices. Make sure any flowers bought at greenhouses are free of insecticides, especially systemic ones which contaminate the nectar even after hosing the leaves. And if you're trying to make your yard attractive to birds, don't lace your lawn with pesticides, or you'll be inviting birds over only to poison them. Remember that birds are illiterate. They can't read those little signs that warn about staying off the grass for forty-eight hours.

## Pet birds at home and school

Traditional pet birds make wonderful companions and can teach children valuable lessons about birds and how they live. Selecting the right one for home or school depends on several factors.

Birds in the parrot family, such as cockatiels and parakeets (more properly called budgerigars or budgies) are adaptable and intelligent but usually work well with children only if they were hand-reared (fed by hand while they were tiny chicks) or hand-tamed (handled frequently while still small). All parrots are sociable creatures who learn vocalizations from one another. A single hand-reared budgie or cockatiel can be perfectly happy without avian companionship but only because it has become imprinted on humans and thus needs a human companion. These single birds readily learn to speak but require a great deal of daily love and attention from one special human. They would get very lonely if left alone for a whole day, so children who choose one should be committed to giving it lots of time and love for the duration of its long life—and these birds have life spans similar to, or longer than, dogs and cats.

The one problem with cockatiels and budgies is that they learn to imitate more sounds than just speech—yours may learn to whistle or screech, especially if it doesn't get enough attention.

Budgerigars and cockatiels are both native to Australia, a country that enforces strict regulations protecting its native birds. Those sold here have been raised in captivity for many generations, so there is no question that budgies and cockatiels on the market are genuinely domesticated, not kidnaped from the wild. Also, because they are from Australia, they are

### Birds in schools

Classroom teachers should only consider getting a single cockatiel or budgie if they have the time and commitment to bring it home each weekend, holiday, and vacation. A pair of birds can be left over the weekend.

**Pet birds**

- cockatiel
- budgerigar
- lovebird
- zebra finch
- canary
- mynah
- duckling
- European starling

adapted to a broad range of environmental conditions and cope well with the temperature and humidity ranges found in most homes and schools. Many larger parrots are from the tropics and may be more susceptible to pneumonia and other respiratory ailments. Also, some parrots are still being stolen from the wild. Large parrots are too expensive for most children to afford anyway.

ESPECIALLY FOR GROUPS

Classroom teachers who prefer birds that can be left alone on weekends and can be sent home with volunteer children on vacations and for the summer have several choices. A pair of budgies or cockatiels will keep each other company, and sometimes may still learn to speak. Since they eat seeds which are dry and don't spoil, they can be left at school over the weekend. Lovebirds cope well in pairs, too, but make loud, screechy calls that are too distracting in a classroom. Some lovebirds also bite harder than their name would suggest.

Zebra finches are easy to keep, make soft, pleasant beeping sounds rather than loud whistles, and often breed in captivity, even in fairly small cages. They won't interact with children the way a bird in the parrot family will but are great fun to watch. Make sure you get a good book about caring for them because children are sad when eggs don't hatch or baby finches die. Also, unless you are careful about food and nest materials, a female may get egg-bound and die.

Canaries make beautiful but distracting music—especially males searching for a mate or proclaiming territorial rights against other males. Canaries interact with children more than zebra finches do but less than small parrots.

Mynahs are interesting and adaptable but are large fruit eaters requiring daily feeding and cleaning. They can also be very noisy. The European Starling is closely related to the mynah and often learns to speak. It's a wild bird but it isn't protected by law because it's not native to America. You can sometimes get a baby starling from someone who runs a bluebird trail or has flicker boxes—most trail managers toss out starling eggs and nestlings. My son Joey wanted a pet bird when he was in first grade, so I asked a friend who maintains bluebird and flicker boxes to save me a baby starling. That was seven years ago. Our Mortimer makes all kinds of lovely sounds, plus he imitates a whistling tea kettle and our smoke detector, but he's never learned to talk. He's been a fine addition to our family but requires daily feeding and attention from us. To keep a starling in a classroom, a teacher would need to make provisions for its care every weekend and holiday.

It's fun to hatch chick or duck eggs in an incubator and raise the babies for a while. If you do this, make sure you study and follow the procedures for turning the eggs and keeping them moist, or some of the babies may hatch with serious deformities that will make everyone sad. Also, make sure ahead of time that you have a place to bring the babies to once they've grown too big to keep in the classroom.

Ducklings are a better choice than chicks because of the chicken social structure. "Pecking order" is a literal term—even the tiniest, cutest chicks establish their order in the group by pecking at one another. In this system, bullies are rewarded, and the meek not only don't inherit the earth—they usually get crushed into it. The weakest baby is often pecked to death, sometimes right in front of horrified little kids. Ducklings are much more fun and are more likely than chickens to be welcomed to a farm where they won't be butchered.

If even one child is allergic, uncomfortable levels of dust will accumulate if you keep birds for long periods, but you can still provide brief visits from living birds. Classroom teachers can ask a local zoo docent, naturalist, or other resource person to visit. Falconers are often happy to bring their raptors to schools. When I take Sneakers, my licensed education Blue Jay, to classrooms, children are transfixed. Sneakers can keep even the most restless kindergartners spellbound for an hour. As long as she's there for a reasonably short time and allergic children don't get too close, she doesn't cause any problems.

Many of today's prominent ornithologists first became interested in birds when they were children, while raising a pet crow or jay. It's often love for an individual that ignites learning and then concern about whole populations. Pet birds at home or in the classroom may be a lot of work, but they have the power to touch children's minds, hearts, and souls like little else—except maybe a puppy.

## Wild birds in the classroom

It is against federal and state laws to rehabilitate birds without a license. The U.S. Fish and Wildlife Service is charged with the responsibility of protecting native birds and enforcing the Migratory Bird Act. Current regulations prohibit even licensed bird rehabilitators from displaying birds under their care, so teachers, even those with rehabilitation licenses, can no longer legally take care of hurt or orphaned birds at school.

As a licensed rehabilitator and a mother, I've had wonderful opportunities to provide my children with wild bird experiences that few modern children ever receive. My kids have helped me raise and successfully release baby Blue Jays, robins, flickers, Cedar Waxwings, Pine Siskins, Common Nighthawks, and other species. Thanks to these close encounters, Joey, Katie, and Tommy have developed an extraordinary level of empathy and compassion for wild creatures and sound knowledge of how to help them. But these riches have come at a steep price—many times my kids have been heartbroken watching me struggle to save endearing little birds that died despite our hard work and knowledge. We've lost opportunities for vacations and other fun activities because I've been tied down with responsibilities during "baby bird season." Caring for a baby bird requires feedings three times an hour during daylight for two or three weeks and another month or two of guarding and tending to the baby outside as it develops the skills it needs to be wild. Inexperienced people who raise baby birds and then simply release them in the woods have essentially condemned their bewildered little charges to a cruel death of starvation or predation. Parents willing to get the training and make the commitment to do rehabilitation properly will be richly rewarded, but this is far more than a hobby and shouldn't be entered into lightly.

Occasionally rehabilitators treat birds that have imprinted on humans or have permanent injuries that won't heal sufficiently for successful release. These birds must be euthanized or brought to a licensed educational facility. Many birds, including virtually all songbirds, have fixed behavior patterns and are unsuited to captivity except in large zoo aviaries. But in rare cases, smaller birds of prey and imprinted crows or jays may make wonderful additions to a classroom. If a teacher has the interest and expertise, it may be possible to obtain a special permit to possess one or two of these unreleasable wild birds for educational purposes. Parents and grandparents are not allowed to possess wild birds to educate just their own children—this is no different from keeping a pet, and it is prohibited by law.

When I was a classroom teacher, students sometimes brought hurt birds or what they believed were orphaned baby birds to school. At that time, licensed rehabilitators weren't prohibited from showing injured and baby birds to the public, so I brought my avian charges to school if they needed attention during the day. Whenever we had a bird in the classroom, the kids were wonderfully quiet and gentle. Virtually every child has an enormous capacity for empathy and compassion, and it's surprisingly easy to elicit these tender feelings when a small animal is involved. My students took turns with baby bird duty—every fifteen minutes someone quietly got up and fed the babies. By summer vacation, most of the babies were fledglings, ready to be released in my yard at a time when I was in a position to feed and protect them as they developed the skills to become properly wild.

As much fun as it was, the enormous amount of work involved in raising baby birds taught the kids that parent birds really are more suited to the task than we mere humans are. The kids quickly learned that when they found a *fledgling* (a bird that has hopped out of the nest on its own, like a two-year-old human climbing out of a crib) the appropriate thing is to set it in a nearby bush or tree where it can attract its parents with begging calls. If they found a *nestling* (a still helpless baby bird that has been knocked from its nest by high wind or an accident), they learned to do their best to get it back into the nest. Parent birds recognize their babies the way we humans do, by sight and sound rather than odor, and readily take care of their own baby after human hands return it to their nest. (For information about how to help a baby bird in an emergency, see Chapter 8.)

Once a Brown Creeper with a concussion and a minor wing sprain spent four days at school. We fed it mealworms, and the kids brought fresh branches for it to climb in search of tiny bugs. I keep very few injured birds in cages, where they may damage flight feathers against the bars, and this one was calm enough to keep loose in the room. (Some people worry about taming birds, but in the case of injured adult songbirds that won't be kept in captivity long, I've found that the more safe and comfortable they feel with us, the better their prognosis. They remain perfectly wild, never returning to us after being released.) This little creeper spent much of its time creeping up trouser legs and knee socks, and the children were charmed. When it was sufficiently recovered, we brought it to a nearby woodlot and released it. We were all proud of ourselves for helping it, happy that it was free, relieved that we didn't need to follow it with toilet paper anymore, and sad that we would never see it again. For

homework, I had them write an essay explaining the meaning of the word *ambivalence*.

In our classroom, we also once cared for a Cedar Waxwing that had become intoxicated after eating fermented mountain ash berries. Waxwings are extraordinarily sociable, and this one wouldn't eat when left alone, so I kept it on my shoulder most of the three days it was with us and even took it to a faculty meeting one afternoon. Waxwings have such lovely, sleek plumage that they look almost artificial, and everyone apparently thought this was a carving I'd pinned to my shoulder until the principal made an emphatic point, and the waxwing turned its head sharply to stare at her. She let out a scream that still rings in my ears.

Wild birds in the classroom do pose serious difficulties. The most adaptable species are also the messiest, requiring daily cleaning. They also require daily feedings of fresh, spoilable food, so somebody has to either go to the school or bring the bird home every weekend and holiday, and even on unexpected "snowdays." Many wild birds can also be noisy distractions. The typical pet birds can teach many of the same lessons, so only consider getting a permit to keep a wild bird if you have a real commitment to providing both a unique experience to your students and a high-quality life for the bird entrusted to your care.

accipiter

buteo

eagle

harrier

osprey

falcon

# 4

# BIRD IDENTIFICATION STARTERS

People like to know the names of things—that's the way we are. Children are no exception. When they see a bright red, crested bird, they aren't satisfied to call it a "Bright-red Crested Bird." They want to know its real name—the name adults call it. Learning the names of birds also makes people of all ages more aware of the enormous variety of species, individualizing them. A person who recognizes thirty different warblers will be more knowledgeable and concerned about those that are threatened or endangered than a person who thinks of warblers as a generic term for common forest birds. So learning bird identification has important conservation implications. Children absorb vocabulary, including complicated words, incredibly quickly—consider how fast a three-year-old masters the names of dinosaurs—so the huge variety of species isn't as daunting to them as it may seem to us.

According to many paleontologists and to the movie *Jurassic Park*, there isn't much difference between birds and dinosaurs. Luckily for tiny paleontologists, dinosaurs are a lot easier to master than birds. For one thing, dinosaurs exist today only in books, toys, and movies, where they hold still long enough for little ones to see the terrible claw on *Deinonychus*, the three horns on *Triceratops*, and the nostrils atop the head of *Brachiosaurus*. Birds flutter about, hide in trees, and dive under water, making field study, especially with small kids, frustrating. And bird books, especially field guides, offer so many choices that it's hard to find the right page while the bird is still in view. For most (but not all) preschoolers, field guides are pretty much worthless.

## Get the picture

So what's a parent, teacher, or naturalist to do? The easiest way to begin learning bird identification is with posters and pictures cut from nature magazines or old bird books. They can be mounted on cardboard and laminated for durability. Clear self-adhesive plastic shelf liner also works well to protect pictures and flash cards.

Magazine photos are large, beautiful, and often show birds doing interesting things. They can be used as springboards to discuss all kinds of topics, from bird behavior to color recognition. Field guide illustrations are smaller and less visually exciting, but they show birds in the simplest, most straightforward poses to make identification easier.

Whether you prefer large photos or small field guide illustrations, select species kids are likely to find nearby, those with historical, social, aesthetic, or practical significance to them, or simply those they want to learn about. You can make a family or classroom field guide booklet, including pictures of birds the children are likely to see or have already seen. Children can write captions with their own observations about noticeable characteristics and behaviors, and they will be thrilled to add new species now and then. A family can continue to develop this book over many years as a lasting record of birds they've enjoyed together, even adding snapshots taken by parents and children.

One of my teacher friends makes a simple set of flash cards for each child by photocopying black-and-white drawings. Kids can color these to reinforce learning. She makes transparencies to use with an overhead projector for quick reviews and quizzes.

It's even easier to mount pictures from an old field guide on index cards to serve as flash cards. If you reserve one falling-apart field guide for cutting up, every American species will be available. Don't do the whole book at once; simply select species that are of immediate interest. These flash cards work great for advanced birders, too, especially for reviewing difficult groups like warblers and shorebirds or for study before going to a new region of the country. No matter what kind of flash cards you make, it's easy to construct a poster with paper pockets to hold twenty or so flash cards for a wall or bulletin board display. The flash cards on the next two pages can be photocopied and will give you a start with some of the most common species.

## Real birds guaranteed to hold still

Live birds at a nearby feeder or natural area obviously provide the most gratifying and exciting new experiences for young birders, and even the most urban setting will have pigeons, starlings, and a few other species. Many zoos have aviaries with native birds. But it's possible to teach an in-depth, richly interesting identification lesson without ever seeing a living bird. Nature centers, colleges, and natural history museums often display showcases of mounted birds. These specimens were prepared by taxidermists to hold life-like poses, and the best museums display them in appropriate habitat panoramas. Museum displays offer a bonus—you can get information from staff ahead of time, so if bird identification isn't your strong suit, you won't be worried about making mistakes. Mounted birds give children accurate size comparisons between species and are a wonderful starting point for playing search games with a field guide. Unfortunately, feathers accumulate dust and may fade slightly with time, so birds in older collections may appear duller than their corresponding field guide pictures.

# FLASH CARD FUN

Blue Jay                    Starling

Crow                       Chickadee

© Pfeifer-Hamilton Publishers • 210 West Michigan • Duluth, MN 55810          (218) 727-0500

# FLASH CARD FUN

Red-winged Blackbird

Robin

Pigeon

House Sparrow

© Pfeifer-Hamilton Publishers • 210 West Michigan • Duluth, MN 55810          (218) 727-0500

Dead birds, even in lifelike poses, evoke sad feelings in many children. Long ago, collectors shot birds just to display them, which offends the sensibilities of most modern people. Discussions about current laws that protect birds often help children to overcome this sadness. Once it became against the law for individuals to possess native bird specimens, would it have been better to throw mounted birds in the garbage or give them to museums so people could learn from them? Thought-provoking questions such as this may lead to stimulating discussions that go far beyond identification.

"Study specimens" look not just merely dead but really most sincerely dead. Cotton stuffing shows through the eye holes of these little corpses which are kept in clear plastic tubes in morguelike drawers. These specimens are found in biology departments of colleges and universities and in teaching rather than public areas of museums. Some professors and curators are reluctant to allow children to see, much less handle, study specimens, which hold enormous ornithological value, but other scientists are eager to share their work with children, even encouraging them to learn the proper way to handle these irreplaceable specimens.

Every study specimen bears a tag on its leg which includes the exact date when the bird was killed, the location, and the bird's age, sex, and cause of death. Some specimens still in use were prepared in the 1800s. Older specimens generally were shot ("collected" in museum jargon), but more recent ones were virtually all killed at picture windows, radio and TV towers, or by cats or automobiles.

Study specimens hold endless possibilities for fascinating study. They can be used to show plumage differences, especially between close relatives like Hairy and Downy Woodpeckers, and to provide close-up observations of difficult groups like sparrows and warblers. Turn specimens of male hummingbirds at different angles to see the glowing color change of the iridescent throat feathers. Bill shape, foot structure, and delicate feather patterns are all plainly visible on study specimens. These features often reveal more than identification—they may give clues to food preferences and habitat requirements. Many bird artists use study specimens to see plumage details clearly and to match colors exactly.

## Finding birds in field guides

The whole point behind learning bird identification is for children to be able to figure out real birds on their own. The smallest children are happy to take your word for the names of birds and are good at remembering which one is the chickadee and which the junco, but as they get older they become eager to figure out new birds all by themselves. This is when they need to learn how to use a field guide.

The first time children handle a field guide, give them time to scan through it, savoring the rich assortment of North American birds. With little kids, you might search for a bird of each color or find the funniest, prettiest, ugliest, most colorful, drabbest, and weirdest species. If you've made flash cards or have magazine pictures available, see how many the children can match in their guide.

Since field guides arrange birds in a loose taxonomic order, species that look very much alike, yet are not at all related, may be far apart in a guide. Have kids use the index to find the Common Loon, Mallard, and American Coot. These ducklike birds are placed far apart in field guides because, despite their similar shapes, they aren't at all related. The Black Phoebe and Dark-eyed Junco have identical slate-gray upper sides, white tummies, and white outer tail feathers. Look at the range maps and their posture and bill shape to guess how bird-watchers tell the two apart. Why do you think they belong to different families?

Look at the many colors birds can be. How many shades of red, blue, and brown can you find? An ordinary Blue Jay is black, white, gray, and several shades of blue, from a soft

**Is Woodstock a warbler?**

When I asked Charles Schulz what species Woodstock is, he wrote, "He and Snoopy have never been able to figure out what kind of a bird he is." Schulz reminded me that Woodstock "was originally a girl bird, for she was Snoopy's secretary."

lavender on the back to deep blue on the tail and wings. Compare the bright colors of the adult male Painted Bunting with the drab colors of the female. Which one can sit on eggs without alerting a predator? Usually when species show such strong differences between the sexes, the female is the one to incubate, but male Rose-breasted Grosbeaks not only help incubate, they sometimes sing at full volume while sitting on the nest!

For fun, try to find close approximations to cartoon birds in the field guide. Friend Owl in *Bambi* and the owl in *Sleeping Beauty* are easy to recognize—they're obviously patterned on Great Horned Owls. Disney crows and ravens are trickier. With their yellow or orange bills, their front half actually resembles a relative of crows and ravens, the Yellow-billed Magpie. I wrote to the Disney Archives for an explanation. It turns out the artists had never heard of a Yellow-billed Magpie. They answered, "Yellow or orange with black is a striking color combination. Black, as a neutral, sometimes gets lost in the shadows. By putting a very bright orange/yellow next to it, it doesn't get lost." Ward Kimball, the Disney artist who animated the crows in *Dumbo*, said, "We exercise artistic license, and yellow looks very good with black. We're not ornithologists, and we go with whatever looks good and reads best against our backgrounds."

How closely does Roadrunner resemble a real Greater Roadrunner? What might Big Bird be, or Gonzo the Muppet? Some people dispute that Gonzo is a bird at all, even if he is in love with a flock of chickens. There are obviously no right or wrong answers. Kids may come up with all kinds of hybrid possibilities for these imaginary birds and have lots of fun as they grow comfortable looking through a field guide.

Most field guides have a page near the beginning illustrating the *topography*, or parts, of a bird. On page 78 of this book you will find a topographical diagram that can be photocopied. Ask the children to find as many of these parts as they can on specimens and pictures. A good exercise is to draw the bird, including as many features as they can see, then put away the specimen or photo and, using only their description and drawing, try to find it in the field guide. This activity not only builds observation powers, but also nurtures field skills required by professional ornithologists and field birders.

## What to look for

Bird identification is based on many characteristics, some obvious and some subtle. Over 700 species live in North America, with most states listing at least 300 species on their official bird rosters. Some, like the Blue Jay and cardinal, are easy to recognize but others are less distinctive. Some can be determined only by a clear look at obscure field marks, and a few species are identical in plumage, differing only in their songs.

Nonbirding parents and teachers (and sometimes even general naturalists) often feel overwhelmed by the number of bird species, afraid that only an experienced bird-watcher or ornithologist is qualified to teach bird identification when there are so many possibilities for error. But if you do make a mistake now and then, what's the big deal? Even a complete novice can help kids recognize and enjoy the birds around them, and learning bird identification together makes the experience for kids richer in many ways than when an expert adult simply dispenses the information.

When identifying a new bird, shapes and proportions of the whole body and of specific parts such as the bill, wings, and tail are critical, particularly for figuring out to which family it belongs. Posture is also important. The Golden field guide does an especially good job of showing shape differences between birds, with silhouettes on many pages to compare similar groups.

Color and plumage patterns help once you have a bird narrowed down to family or genus. In the field, behaviors such as flight patterns and feeding techniques give important clues, and songs and calls are often diagnostic. Habitat will help in

**Bird silhouettes**
You can draw silhouettes on black construction paper and cut them out for study—these are especially helpful for learning hawk identification and make wonderful window decorations. (Hawk silhouettes, when taped to picture windows, may have the added benefit of warning smaller birds away, so they don't smack into the window.)

many cases, and so field guide illustrators draw many birds in appropriate habitat. But during migration, birds can end up in odd places—once a Sora (a kind of marsh bird) was filmed on the sidelines of a nationally broadcast football game—a habitat you won't find illustrated in field guides. Size is probably the least useful characteristic for identification, especially for unfamiliar birds in flight. Against the sky, it's hard to be sure whether we're looking at something big and far away or something small and nearby. Experienced birders and even professional hawk counters have been known to look twice, and even three times, at a dragonfly or airplane before realizing it's not a bird.

In urban settings, mallards, pigeons, swifts, chickadees, crows, robins, starlings, and sparrows may all be seen on a short walk. I've taken my Madison, Wisconsin, junior-high classes on fifty-minute walks and discovered thirty or more species. But the birds we found were widely separated in the field guides, so it's important that beforehand children become at least a little familiar with the many possibilities.

**Practice makes perfect**

Remember that even well-prepared people—adults as well as kids—may find looking up real live birds in the book tricky at first. When I set out on my first birding expedition in March 1975 it took me about an hour of traipsing around a university woodlot to finally find a single bird, but the one that appeared turned out to be unusually cooperative. As it flitted around me, I searched through the guide, beginning with the loons, and finally found a page with birds looking like mine. Just in case there might be similar birds elsewhere in the book, I checked every page all the way to the end and then came back to the likely suspects. Two looked absolutely identical, but according to the field guide, they could be distinguished by voice and range. I was using the Golden guide, which doesn't include state lines on the range maps, and wasn't quite sure whether I was near the southern end of one range or the northern end of the other. So I listened hard to my cooperative little subject and then went to the university library to listen to bird recordings, where I finally made my first positive bird identification—a Black-capped Chickadee.

Two months later, in May, I was feeling more confident, and one morning decided I no longer needed to go through the whole book for every single new bird. When I found a tiny yellow bird warbling away in a spruce tree, I went straight to the warblers. There are dozens of pages of warblers, and after poring over them three times, I still couldn't find my bird, so I went back to my tried-and-true method of checking out every single possibility—this one proved to be an American Goldfinch. I felt discouraged, but little by little, I became better at noticing important field marks like bill and tail shape. By the end of my first spring as a bird-watcher, I had identified only forty species, but boy did I know those forty well! And I also knew my Golden guide cover to cover—soon I could find just about any bird in less than ten seconds.

## Learning to look

Dozens of activities can help children practice identification skills. For example, after distributing magazine photos or study specimens, ask kids to look at their bird's basic field marks. You might ask questions such as the following: How big is the bird in relation to a sparrow, robin, and crow? (That's hard to tell with a photo—they may have to guess.) What color(s) is it? Describe the color pattern. Is it a solid color? Spotted? Streaked? Mottled? (*Mottled* is a word that applies to many birds. Have someone look up its meaning in a dictionary.) Does it have wingbars? Eye rings? Markings on the breast? Is the *rump* (the base of the tail at the back) or the *crissum* (the base of the tail at the belly) a contrasting color? What shape is the beak? How long is the beak compared to the head? How

**U.F.O.'s**

Remember that not even experienced birders recognize every bird they see, and some species are very tricky. There will be many "ones that got away." We can imagine those "U.F.O.'s" are Ivory-billed Woodpeckers and Passenger Pigeons.

long is the tail compared to the body? Is the tail tip round, square, or pointed?

Because study specimens are prepared in such a dramatically unlifelike pose, finding these birds in field guides can be challenging at first, but taking the time to search through a guide is often fun and always helpful in developing identification skills.

### The sound of music

When I go on a bird walk on a spring morning, I may end up with a list of eighty species even though I've seen only sixty. Experienced birders recognize birds by song and are perfectly satisfied listing "heard only" birds on a daily checklist. After all, some birds' songs are far more impressive than their plumage. The tiny, drab Winter Wren sings one of the longest, loveliest of all bird songs. Hearing an ethereal, flutelike thrush song ringing through the woods is far more joyful than merely looking at the dull singer.

From CDs or records, dub a cassette tape of five or ten bird songs that children are most likely to hear in your area. (Remember, this is legal fair use only if you own the CDs or records or, in the case of library loans, if you erase the tapes when you return the recordings.) Once the kids have mastered a few calls, tape five or ten new ones. Spice up the tape now and then with silly or lovely songs. Don't forget the Willow Ptarmigan (available on *Peterson Western Bird Songs*)—it's about as silly as you can get. If a bird is mentioned in a story the kids are reading, add its call to your tape. Set aside a moment each morning for a "bird song of the day."

The song of the American Robin is one of the most important to learn for comparison purposes. It sings a long, fluted "sentence" composed of "words" of two or three syllables. The Red-eyed Vireo's tone quality is very robinlike, but it's called the preacher bird because it drones on and on throughout the day, pausing as if for dramatic emphasis between words.

Rose-breasted and Black-headed Grosbeaks sound like robins who've had voice training, with richer, throatier tones. The Scarlet Tanager sounds like a robin with a sore throat—raspy and burry. By matching songs and descriptions, little by little the kids will figure out the ways we describe songs, and they will develop listening skills that will help when they encounter an unfamiliar song in the field.

Pictures, books, museums, and recordings provide countless learning opportunities, but the real joy of bird identification study obviously comes from living, breathing birds. By the time children recognize several common species by sight and sound and feel comfortable using a field guide, they, and you, will be eager to get outside and practice these skills in the real world. It's time to go birding.

**Fun with bird songs**

Read the descriptions of recorded songs before playing them. See if the kids can come up with word phrases that remind them of the rhythm patterns of songs. For example:

- Birders often remember the Barred Owl's call by the phrase, "Who cooks for you? Who cooks for you all?"
- The White-throated Sparrow sings "Old Sam Peabody, Peabody, Peabody, Peabody," at least up to the Canadian border, where it changes its tune to "Oh, sweet Canada, Canada, Canada, Canada."
- Yellow Warblers sing, "Sweet, sweet, sweet. Aren't I so sweet?"
- Song Sparrows sing, "Zing, zing, zizzy, zizzy, zing, zing."

# 5

## PLANNING BIRD OUTINGS WITH KIDS

irding with children can be a boom or bust activity depending on location, time of year, weather, and just plain luck. Some of the most well-laid-out plans for quality birding adventures in prime locations can be rained or snowed out. One short walk around a city block can be filled with chirping sparrows, starlings perched atop every chimney, and pigeons waddling about on the sidewalks, or it may seem as if every single bird hightailed it out of the county for the day. So providing quality outdoor experiences for children requires flexible plans and a sense of humor.

Remember, too, that what's wonderful and exciting for adults may be downright unpleasant for kids. On a family drive to New England in 1993, we stopped en route in Grayling, Michigan, to see Kirtland's Warblers. I spent much of the 500-mile drive telling my children about this fascinating "bird of fire," who nests on the ground beneath young jack pines after fire has cleared old forest and germinated the jack pine cones. I made them read a booklet about Kirtland's Warbler, and I knew they would be thrilled to see this unique species. We arrived at our motel after midnight so they were groggy and out-of-sorts when I woke them at 6 A.M. for our tour.

**Birding for kids**

Enthusiastic birders often desperately want their children to share their passion, but have to be careful not to drag them to one too many sewage ponds. If you don't want to turn kids off to birds, make sure the birding opportunities you provide are really for them and not for you.

Kirtland's Warbler is an endangered species, and the U.S. Forest Service protects it by keeping people out of breeding areas except on official tours. We watched the required video with a ranger and then set out. By mid-morning, the late June sun and hot, muggy air sapped us of energy and enthusiasm. I heard over a dozen Kirtland's Warblers, but we didn't see a single one for over three hours when one finally lighted in a bush and allowed me a clear view for about three seconds. The kids got a split-second glimpse as it flew across an opening at high speed, and my husband didn't see it at all. And that was that. The kids were pretty polite about the experience, but on the rest of the drive to Maine, whenever I talked about showing them Atlantic Puffins, they gave each other surreptitious, helpless glances and politely said "Sure, Mom."

ESPECIALLY FOR GROUPS

## Make the most of serendipitous opportunities

Some of the best birding experiences I've had with children were spur of the moment. One spring morning right as I was starting to hand out a math test to my seventh graders, a large kettle of Broad-winged Hawks swirling in the blue sky outside the window caught my eye. Almost all the kids were unprepared for this particular test because their intramural team had unexpectedly been invited to play in a tournament the night before. I normally held rigidly to scheduled test dates, but this was a unique case on two fronts—sports and birds—and I still remember how their faces glowed with relief when I asked if anyone would mind terribly if I postponed the test a day so we could spend this hour outside, quantifying migration and drawing graphs. I suspect one or two of them may still harbor warm feelings toward Broad-winged Hawks for that reprieve.

Every birding experience you have on your own will add to your competence and increase your enjoyment of outings with children. Take advantage of local bird club meetings and field trips, where you will meet friendly and knowledgeable birders and get a good feel for field identification. You'll also learn techniques for pointing out birds to large groups and tips on how to find things quickly with binoculars and spotting scopes. Teachers might send notes to parents publicizing some of these field trips so interested children and their families may also attend.

A fifth-grade teacher brought a couple of his students along with my group on a Christmas Bird Count. At first he seemed nervous that the kids might mess up the day for serious adults in the group, but the children's keen eyes found several birds we grown-ups hadn't noticed, and their enthusiasm and sense of fun made the day more enjoyable than it would have been without them. He had prepared them ahead of time so they were dressed for the weather and came with plenty of nutritious food.

One Duluth fifth-grade class saved money and "adopted" an owl at Hawk Ridge Nature Reserve's banding station. One of the benefits of adopting an owl at this facility is an invitation to watch the banding operation, but because the station is small and can manage only a handful of people at a time, Hawk Ridge must limit visitors. The teacher held a drawing to determine which child would come with her—the winner was required to make a full report to the class about the experience. The lucky student's dad photographed everything that happened: the boy placed his ear on the back of a Saw-whet Owl to listen to its heartbeat, and he held and released the class's official adopted owl. The rest of the children obviously didn't have as wonderful an experience as he did, but everyone learned a lot about owls and banding, and several other children talked their families into adopting owls so they could observe banding firsthand, too.

**Christmas Bird Count**

The Christmas Bird Count has been an annual tradition since 1900. Most cities in the United States and Canada have an official count. Participants spend the day searching out and counting every bird they can within a 15-mile diameter "count circle." Data from every count is compiled by the National Audubon Society in their journal, *Audubon Field Notes*. The cost of printing this enormous annual volume is paid by a small participation fee.

To connect with the nearest CBC, call your local or state bird club.

**Why did the Hollywood chicken cross the road?** Because she wanted to see Gregory peck.

Some nature centers and college biology departments employ licensed banders who may be willing to allow a few students to watch their operations. But opportunities like these aren't always publicized—become a member of your nearest nature center or bird club to find out what special experiences might be available.

Remember that kids aren't welcome at some birding events. It is inappropriate for children to participate in Breeding Bird Surveys, Christmas Bird Counts, or other data-collecting situations unless they are both mature and motivated—otherwise the scientific value of the survey could be compromised. Some experiences require participants to remain silent for many minutes or even hours, concentrating on birds and nothing else.

But don't underestimate a motivated child's capabilities. I spent one cold March evening in an observation blind at the Lillian Annette Rowe Audubon Sanctuary in Nebraska watching vast numbers of Sandhill Cranes fly in to rest on the Platte River at sunset. Sanctuary visitors who observe cranes from this blind are required to stay (without access to a bathroom) for almost three hours, from late afternoon until after dark, so the birds won't be disturbed by human activity—after all, this is a sanctuary for birds, not for people. Children under eight aren't allowed in the blind, but there were three slightly older children in our group. As might be expected, there was an awful lot of annoying fidgeting, giggling, and talking, but it was all done by a few adults in the group. The children behaved perfectly.

When my husband and I brought our three children to Machias Seal Island off the coast of Maine to see Atlantic Puffins and other seabirds, a professional nature photographer gave the kids disparaging looks on the boat ride to the island. He was obviously annoyed that he had picked a day when kids were along to scare the birds away. But as he saw how interested, knowledgeable, and well-behaved they were, both on the boat and in the blinds, he ended up praising them for being fine company. (By the way, on the island the kids came within inches of puffins and other exciting birds, and they had a fantastic time. Arranging this trip fully redeemed me after the Kirtland's Warbler fiasco.)

## When and where to go

Your geographic location will help you figure out the best times of year and places to go for bird-watching. Some areas, such as just about any wetland in Florida, are rich in approachable bird life year-round. Others have annual rhythms that include periods when birds are few and far between. Certain localities enjoy unique natural events that shouldn't be wasted: spring and/or fall hawk migration along mountain ranges and shores; waterfowl nesting and migration in lakes, ponds, and ocean coastlines; early spring Sandhill Crane migration along the Platte River, Whooping Cranes wintering near Corpus Christi, spring displays of grouse or prairie chickens in expansive grasslands, or swans wintering on the Chesapeake Bay. The more you learn about your own area's birding potential, the more opportunities you can take advantage of.

Some general rules about timing: spring birds tend to be more conspicuous than fall or winter birds because males sing most during the breeding season when they also display their fanciest plumage. Ducks, geese, and swans often return in spring just as ice is melting, weeks before songbirds return. Spring movements begin much earlier in the south than the north—in the upper Midwest, the first day of spring doesn't look much different from the first day of winter. Well-stocked feeders at nature centers and similar places may attract a wide variety of birds during any season, but are usually most exciting during migration and winter.

Decisions about the timing of trips should take into account the children's well-being. Where the weather gets extremely hot or cold, it may be wise to limit birding units to seasons with moderate temperatures. But don't be too rigid.

**Why didn't the chicken cross the road?**

Because she was chicken.

**Why did the Blue Jay cross the road?**

Because she wasn't chicken.

**Travel on the Internet**

On the Internet, students can share their discoveries with classes from other latitudes, learning a wealth of information about the differences and similarities between distant landscapes and habitats while reinforcing their knowledge about their own area.

Classes at Toivola-Meadowlands School in northern Minnesota help on the annual Christmas Bird Count during a month when daily high temperatures are often well below zero. These children get to see Great Gray Owls and other exciting species from their heated school bus, and their participation also makes a valuable contribution to our understanding of avian population trends.

One of my friends takes interested fifth graders out once a week during spring to watch for signs of spring. They start when snow and ice dominate the landscape and watch the changes from week to week, maintaining a phenology chart. The kids learn about more than bird identification—they discover that the first ducks to return are divers, followed by the dabblers; birds associated with water return before woodland birds; and early warbler movements are tied to swarming insects over water and to the sudden opening of tiny green leaves. (Warblers fuel their migration on emerging aquatic insects and on newly-hatched caterpillars that eat soft leaf tissue before it can develop cell walls.) The kids' enthusiasm and eagerness to discover new arrivals keep interest in this optional after-school activity high.

**Look for local resources**

To find out about the natural events of your area, read a local phenology book—that will tell you when natural events such as migration, flowers opening, and birds nesting occur from year to year. Also, get a copy of the "birder's guide" and annotated checklist for your state (see Appendix III). Migration and other natural patterns vary from location to location and even from year to year, so phenology books can't possibly predict the exact date on which natural events will occur, but they do give a good idea of what to expect, making it possible to plan activities when bird life is likely to be interesting.

To learn about places in your county and state that are rich in birdlife, check birders' guides, travel books, and your state department of natural resources. When planning long trips, you may want to select destinations with shelters where you can substitute indoor activities if the weather turns nasty.

## Outings to nature centers and zoos

Many local facilities offer special opportunities to observe, and sometimes even handle, birds up close. Nature centers and environmental learning centers sometimes provide classes by licensed bird banders who show children how birds are netted, banded, recorded, and released. This experience will long be remembered, especially if the bander has empathy for both birds and children.

Nature centers and other facilities that rehabilitate injured birds are not allowed to display these birds to the public, but they sometimes have nonreleasable birds that are kept under an educational license for close observation and study. Usually children are not allowed to touch these birds, but in situations where they are, teach them the proper way to pet birds, using two fingers.

Sometimes people who run bluebird trails or other bird nest projects will allow one or two children to accompany them as they check their boxes. Children (and grown-ups) are awestruck when touching a bluebird egg—the warm, alive feeling is unlike anything imaginable. After that experience, even a high-schooler may appreciate reading Dr. Seuss's *Horton Hatches the Egg*.

Zoos may provide special opportunities to handle ducklings or baby chicks. Children's faces light up as they touch these tiny living creatures. But before taking children anywhere to handle or pet small birds, make sure the facility has an ethical policy about the treatment of these animals. When I attended Michigan State University in the mid-1970s, the agriculture college held an annual farm day for children, who were allowed to handle chicks with little supervision. This was obviously hard on the chicks, and because so many of them

**Touching birds**

Most people are inclined to use just their index finger to pet a bird, but this feels like poking to the bird. Tell the children to extend index and middle fingers together. People—including two-year-olds—automatically touch much more gently with the two-finger method.

**Albatross, Bluebird, Chickadee**

On long trips, play car games, such as counting Red-winged Blackbirds or American Kestrels on power lines along the expressway, searching for signs with birds on them, or going through the alphabet looking for birds whose names include each letter. (Good luck with some of those letters—if you don't spot a Fox Sparrow, you may have to be creative and look for some "dux.")

ended up with broken or twisted bones, the policy was to "mercifully" destroy all of them at the end of the day. When area children learned about this, they protested until the university finally stopped the practice. Handling living birds should be a magical experience that sparks a lifetime interest in birds and their protection, so it is critical that adults supervise these experiences with compassion and love for birds and children both.

## Intimate experiences

Going birding with just one or two children is an entirely different experience from going with thirty. When dealing with your own kids or grandkids, you can plan special events that classroom teachers can only dream of, such as evening or midnight walks once a month when the moon is full or sunrise serenades when spring birds are in full song. Birding from a canoe makes for a magical time of beauty and wonder. Leisurely bike rides along country roads can be equally wonderful. During migration, you can point a spotting scope at the moon and watch migrants wing past.

Parents have the luxury of stopping for teachable moments without having to plan the rest of the time—at a beach picnic, you may take a moment to see how terns dive into water for fish while gulls snatch food from the surface, and then go back to tossing the frisbee. On a hike through Yellowstone National Park, our family stopped to watch an American Dipper—a plump, short-tailed robin-sized songbird—walking along the bottom of a rushing mountain stream. The kids were thrilled to see it walk deliberately through a gushing rapids without being swept away. Yet nobody considered the experience a bird walk.

My neighbor, our family's emergency auxiliary backup grandma, used to take her own kids on a "bud walk" in spring when buds were first opening to reveal baby leaves. Migrants appear like magic the day leaves first appear, and birdsong, spring weather, and colorful birds all contributed to make these happy walks linger in her memories.

## Just around the corner

On my daily walks to school, a "cacawphony" of crows more than once alerted me to the presence of a Great Horned Owl—those days my classes abandoned math and took a 15-minute hike to see the owl, making for a jolly outing. My school was a pleasant 10-minute walk from Lake Monona, and when duck migration peaked or on good warbler migration days, I often brought classes there. I'm still grateful to the sympathetic principals who didn't demand that I adhere to lesson plans when there were better things to do.

When good birds appear in my neighborhood and I want to show them to my own kids, I have to remind myself that they aren't being reprieved from math—sometimes they're being snatched from something they really wanted to do more. I want to share birds with them, not impose birds on them. I know I've been striking a good balance when one of them actually comes to me asking me to take them birding.

The more we know about the natural world, the easier it becomes to notice and capitalize on teachable moments and situations that children will really like. Take time once in a while to walk around your neighborhood, figuring out which birds are close enough to find on short walks. Pay particular attention to nearby parks, nature centers, lake access points, sewage ponds (yes, sewage ponds!) and other undeveloped areas, but don't ignore residential and even business zones. A pair of Merlins—little bird-hunting falcons—have nested in a tree across the street from my kids' middle school, right above a heavily used bus stop on a busy road. Killdeer often appear on soccer fields in early spring.

When waves of warblers migrate in May, a rainbow of tiny birds may fill the few trees lining an urban street. Zoos often harbor a great many wild birds on their grounds, especially near ponds and creeks, so a trip to a local zoo can provide close-up looks at both captive and wild birds. And don't overlook the obvious. When I was a graduate student at Michigan State

**Why did the gum cross the road?**

Because it was stuck on the chicken's feet.

**Male or female?**

Many experienced birders don't differentiate between male and female robins, but it isn't difficult. The male's head and back are blackish gray rather than the female's brownish gray, he has more prominent streaking on his throat, and his breast is a richer rust color.

University, I wrote a major paper for an ornithology class comparing House Sparrow feeding behavior at a backyard feeder to how they feed at a McDonald's restaurant.

Robins, cardinals, pigeons, grackles, cowbirds, and sparrows are all interesting to see and identify, and if more exotic species aren't available, you can look closely at common birds for interesting identification studies.

Don't limit walking trips to your immediate neighborhood. Three fifth-grade teachers in my city bring their classes on a six-mile round trip hike to Hawk Ridge Nature Reserve each fall. This is a whole-day outing, with picnic lunch, scheduled visits with naturalists, quantifying and graphing the day's migration, and journal-writing for further enrichment. I sometimes take a five-mile hike with my Katie and Tommy. We eat our picnic lunch at a pleasant spot where we can see several birds and stop along the way whenever we see or hear something interesting, whether it's a bird, a chipmunk, or a hot-air balloon.

**Tricks of the trade**

Remember that both you and children will find more and more birds as you gain experience. During my entire first spring of birding in 1975, I found 40 species. By 1979, I sometimes found more than 100 species in a day, and on one memorable May morning, I found 100 species in a single park in Madison, Wisconsin. Every bird you see makes the next one easier both to find and identify.

Some subtle environmental conditions can make or break a bird outing. In general, birds are most active in early morning and late afternoon. From April through June or early July, when birds are in full song, a dawn walk can be extraordinarily rich. Prior to the walk, play recordings of a few of the most common songs such as those of cardinals and robins so kids will recognize and listen for them.

Singing generally dies down by 9 or 10 A.M. but often

resumes in late afternoon and early evening. During midday, many songbirds rest quietly while activity peaks for daytime migrants such as hawks.

Consider where the sun is in the sky relative to the direction you're walking. Try to walk away from it as much as possible. A vantage point for looking at a lake may face east, perfect for duck-watching in the afternoon but perfectly awful in the morning, when the kids must look directly into the sun.

ESPECIALLY FOR GROUPS

When selecting locations, consider how many children will be coming along. Thirty children walking single-file along a narrow path through even the most beautiful, bird-filled forest are going to miss a lot of birds. Open areas, dirt roads, and wide sidewalks allow kids to bunch up where everyone can see and hear the same things at the same times. Save lovely little pathways for smaller, more intimate teaching situations.

Some children will automatically walk at a faster or slower pace than others. With large groups, make sure there is an adult or leader at the front and at the back and set a rule that everyone must stay between the leaders.

Keep in mind that most children (and adults!) have trouble walking in a group and listening simultaneously. Only the most ardent, motivated birder can concentrate exclusively on birds when friends and other distractions are all around. Sometimes you can instruct kids to look and listen for specific things as you go along, but try to be patient as they relapse into conversations that have nothing to do with your objectives. Unless you're dealing with only two or three kids at a time, it's usually a good idea to approach a bird walk as two separate activities—a fun hike punctuated by stops where everyone concentrates hard on looking and listening for birds. When I go out with my own children on what I consider a

**Windy weather**

Except for some large migrants, birds seldom sing or move about in high winds, so you might as well stay inside on windy days.

**Why did the chicken gobble up the corn?**
Because she was taking revenge on Kernel Sanders.

"bird walk," we invariably spend more than half of the walking time talking about topics completely unrelated to birds.

When using a spotting scope with a group, set the tripod for the height of the shortest person so you won't need to readjust it and relocate the bird for every viewer. Keep the scope mounted on a tripod and ask the children to take turns carrying it as you walk, taking care that the meekest child doesn't end up lugging it the whole way.

Don't overload kids with information on a hike—they'll retain a few pertinent facts much better than a whole litany of bird lore.

During walking time, school teachers may manage groups more easily by giving the kids checklists of things to look for on their own or by designing a scavenger hunt. To make a scavenger hunt more interesting, search for sounds and smells as well as concrete objects. Include behavior categories such as seeing a bird eating a worm, building a nest, or taking a bath. Kids can work independently or in teams.

Scout ahead of time for the best stopping points—locations with large boulders, small hills, or other "natural stages" where you can be seen and heard by everyone. Of course, a good bird may show up between stops, too. There are all kinds of strategies for reengaging children's attention suddenly. Some teachers use a loud whistle or clap their hands in a rhythmic pattern (my best friend uses "shave and a haircut" and the kids must clap back "two bits"). On walks with students or with my Girl Scout troop, I usually bring along an Audubon Bird Call, a little device made of birch-wood and metal that can be twisted to produce various bird sounds. When the kids hear the sound, they know they have to quiet down instantly, or they'll miss something good.

At a stopping point, children may listen for a particular sound, look at a particular bird, or just write observations in their notebooks. You might take a moment to explain something interesting about a bird's behavior or point out identification tips. For example, blackbirds all look pretty much alike at first glance, but check out the beak, eye color, and length of the tail. Starlings (which aren't true blackbirds) are short and dumpy, usually speckled, with yellow beaks. Grackles are long and streamlined, with a long, wedge-shaped tail, a yellow eye, and an iridescent purplish head. Brewer's Blackbirds have the same color pattern as grackles but are shorter and less streamlined. Red-winged Blackbird males are easy to identify, and the females look like oversized sparrows.

Not every bird can be identified. Sometimes we see a bird for too short a time or at the wrong angle to see critical field marks. Some species, such as flycatchers belonging to the genus *Empidonax*, look so similar that they can't be identified with certainty unless they are singing. You may encounter a genuine rarity—a common bird with abnormal plumage colors or patterns or a vagrant that has wandered far from where it belongs. If you see birds you can't identify, don't get discouraged. The more fun you have trying to figure them out, the more contagious your own curiosity and interest will be for the children.

Don't get defensive when you discover that some kids know more than you. I considered myself a top-notch birder before I took a group of seventh graders to my favorite park. One boy suddenly announced that a Prothonotary Warbler had just dropped into the bushes—he was sure of it because it looked just like the picture in the field guide even though he'd never seen a Prothonotary Warbler before. I gently explained that the identification was impossible—I'd been birding in that park almost daily for over three years and had never seen a Prothonotary Warbler there, and besides, it was the wrong habitat. Anyway, without binoculars, he couldn't have seen the bird that well. I suggested that it might have been a Yellow Warbler, and although he looked disappointed, he obviously trusted my judgement.

**Words for bird parts**
Use the chart on the next page to give children a vocabulary for describing birds.

**Birds that misbehave**
Common birds may do odd things quite different from what the field guide says. Remember—we're dealing with a pack of illiterate birds who don't read those books.

# BIRD PARTS

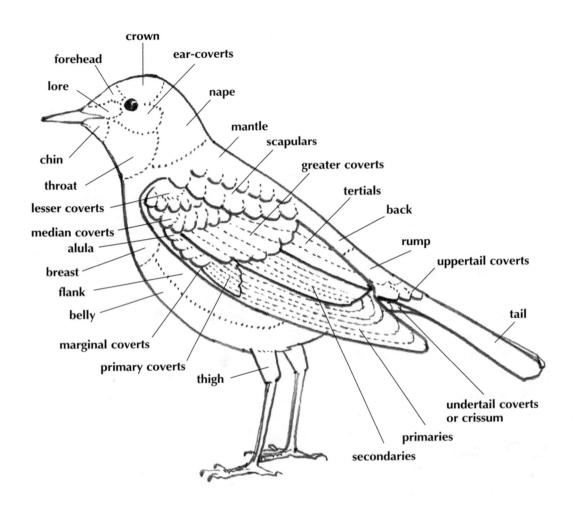

crown
forehead
ear-coverts
lore
nape
mantle
scapulars
greater coverts
tertials
back
chin
rump
throat
uppertail coverts
lesser coverts
median coverts
alula
breast
flank
belly
tail
marginal coverts
primary coverts
thigh
undertail coverts
or crissum
primaries
secondaries

© Pfeifer-Hamilton Publishers  •  210 West Michigan  •  Duluth, MN 55810          (218) 727-0500

Not thirty seconds later the familiar "sweet, sweet, sweet, sweet" of a Prothonotary Warbler rang out from a tree just above where he'd seen it. He was as proud as I was embarrassed.

ESPECIALLY FOR GROUPS

## Looking without binoculars

Ideally, every school in America should have at least one bird unit kit available for teachers to check out, supplied with posters, recordings, local checklists, your area's birder's guide, other resource books (especially John K. Terres's *The Audubon Encyclopedia of North American Birds*), and enough field guides and binoculars to serve a whole classroom. But in the real world, most schools have only a few bird books, kept in the library, and no binoculars at all. Over time, interested teachers collect their own posters, resource books, activity sheets, and other useful materials for bird study. But what about binoculars?

Young eyes are amazingly adept at spotting and observing birds. When I taught junior high, I often invited my students to take the Saturday morning 6 o'clock city bus to my apartment. This was completely optional, without extra credit or other "perks," and although a few kids never took advantage of the opportunity, most of them came at least once or twice, and some showed up every single week. I made waffles for everybody, and then we spent the morning birding. One or two kids invariably brought binoculars, but most didn't have them. When we spotted a bird, we shared what binoculars we had, usually averaging three pairs for 12 people. Often a bird flew away before even half the kids saw it through binoculars, yet most of the time everyone got a decent view thanks to their motivation and keen eyes.

When I took classes on spontaneous bird walks during school, none of the kids had binoculars. Because it took so long to pass the binoculars from child to child, I shared mine

**Vulture humor**

A pair of vultures got sick and tired of flying south on their own power year after year and decided to take a airplane for once. They saved up their money and headed to the airport, but since they'd heard about airplane food, on the way they each found a squashed rabbit in the road and put it in a pouch around their neck to bring along. They bought their tickets, each requesting a window seat in the nonsmoking section. Then the cashier asked if she could check their luggage. They each looked at their pouch and said, "No, thank you. This is carrion."

By the way, did you hear about the maggots that were fighting in dead Ernest?

**Bird humor**

Jay: What has two wings,
an iridescent throat, is
made of cement, and is
the only bird that can fly
backwards?

Robin: I don't know.

Jay: A hummingbird.

Robin: But what about the
cement?

Jay: I just threw that in to
make it hard.

only when we came upon very rare birds that weren't likely to show up again any time soon. I tried to use my binoculars as little as possible when the kids didn't have any. They learned to recognize birds by song as well as plumage, and I, in turn, became less dependent on optical aids.

Sometimes when we rely too much on binoculars, we develop tunnel vision and stop noticing the vast beauty all around. And sometimes we get so keyed in on birds that we miss other forms of natural beauty. Once, my Saturday morning waffle group took a sudden interest in chorus frog calls coming from a puddle in the woods. We sneaked up on them, creeping on our bellies through the mud, stopping whenever they grew silent, and we finally managed to actually see these noisy but shy, inch-long creatures with inflated balloon throats—something we wouldn't have done if everyone was anxiously protecting their parents' binoculars from mud and muck. I made all the kids promise they'd do their own laundry that day.

---

Birders use a few tricks to lure birds in for close observation. A pishing sound—that is, going "Pssshhhh! Pssssshhhh! Pssshhh!"—is very popular with birders. Some ornithologists speculate that the sound may be similar to the fear or hunger calls of fledglings, but it sometimes seems to relieve birder tension more than it attracts birds. The squeaks from Audubon Bird Calls sometimes seem to attract little hawks and owls better than they attract songbirds—too bad there aren't more hawks and owls to attract.

Some professional bird-tour leaders play tape recordings of bird songs to attract territorial males, who may even try to drive the "intruder" away. This is not permitted in some parks and national forests where large number of birders might cause undue stress to rare birds. I never use recordings in the field—it seems an unfair and rude intrusion—but in special circumstances it can be a useful technique if used sparingly and with compassion for the birds' needs. Whistling responses to singing birds often draws them close and somehow seems more fair or at least more sporting than using recordings, plus it's a lot more fun.

The calls of small owls also lure in songbirds—again, I prefer imitations to actual recordings. You can perform the imitation yourself or encourage the kids to learn how. Look at a range map to see which species of screech owl lives in your area or to determine whether you're within the range of the Northern Pygmy-Owl or the Northern Saw-whet Owl. Songbirds try to chase away little owls out of anxiety or fear, so don't use owl calls too often, especially during breeding season.

Like songbirds trying to chase off little owls, big birds try to chase off big owls that might otherwise eat them at nightfall. For this reason, many hawk watch facilities and raptor photographers set out owl decoys to lure in migrating hawks. If you live near a lakeshore, river, or ridgeline where migrating hawks gather, try setting out a plastic owl on a high fence post, the top of a playground slide, or other high point. Taping a few real feathers on it may make it surprisingly effective at bringing migrants close.

Knowing techniques to lure birds in is important when your kids don't have binoculars, but also try to take kids where birds are sure to be. In my own neighborhood and in places where I'm scheduled to lead a field trip for children or adults, I usually look for nests ahead of time. Robin and Chipping Sparrow nests are often easy to find—whenever I see any bird carrying food or nesting materials, I keep patient watch as it makes its way to the nest. Nearby nests are fun to watch with my own kids, but I virtually never show actual nests to groups—that can disturb the birds. Keeping track of these nests allows me to bring people where I know parent birds will be moving about.

**Why do birds fly south for the winter?**

Because it's too far to walk.

**Why does a hummingbird hum?**

Because he doesn't know the words.

Get to know one park or other favorite spot intimately, and you'll start recognizing individual birds and their habits. One spring, I made a bet with my seventh graders that no one could walk one hundred steps down a certain path without ducking or turning back. I had already noticed that the path ran near a Black Tern nest, and sure enough, each child who tried to walk along the path got bombarded. Black Terns aren't kamikaze pilots, and I knew they wouldn't actually bonk into the kids, but they do fly directly toward people's eyes in a most Hitchcockian manner. After trying it themselves, the kids were deeply impressed that I survived without flinching when it was my turn. This technique is a great way to gain the respect of junior high kids—unfortunately, Black Terns only bombard people in spring, when the school year is pretty much over.

**Techniques for pointing out birds**

Probably the trickiest task in leading birding trips for children or adults is pointing out exactly where each bird is. "It's right over there!" "It's straight out from you." "It's in that tree." "It's at one o'clock." These sentences should all be banned from the English language—at least on birding outings. But what do you say when the bird is obviously right over there, straight out from you in that tree at one o'clock?

Sometimes it's possible to use mechanical aids to directly point to birds—a hand mirror reflecting sunlight or a laser gun sight both can be effective (see Chapter 2). But overall, it's more useful to describe locations orally than to depend on these devices.

Telling people where to look to see a bird is a skill that takes time and experience to acquire. Sometimes you or the children will be too excited about a particular bird to be lucid about its location. Whoever is looking at the bird may lose it while putting down binoculars to explain. Sometimes it's in the middle of a tree that looks exactly like every other tree for miles. Sometimes it's perched atop a weed in a field of identical weeds. Birds often fly away before more than one or two people see them—this happens even to experienced professional bird-tour leaders, so don't get discouraged when it happens to you.

Within a vast landscape, describing the particular location of a four-inch bird requires precise language, and an ability to quickly but carefully observe a scene and note the differences between things that seem similar. Saying a bird is "in the oak tree" tells kids a lot more than "it's in that tree" (as long as there's only one oak tree, and as long as the children recognize oaks). "It's halfway down the tallest tree in that stand of conifers, on the right side just below the broken branch," is much more precise than "It's out there at three o'clock." Using the clock as a map is worthless unless everyone with you knows exactly what the plane of your clock is and where twelve o'clock is. Dyslexic children may have enough problems distinguishing their right from their left without also having to picture clockwise and counterclockwise. (I'm dyslexic myself, so I know all about this kind of confusion.) Anyway, many modern children learn to tell time with digital clocks that don't give directional clues at all.

If you bird frequently from a single vantage point—a lakeshore, ridge, playground, or backyard—have the kids look for landmarks that you can always find, such as church steeples, water towers, easily distinguishable houses, noticeable trees, etc. When I went on a birding trip to the Nature Conservancy's Mile Hi Ranch in the Santa Rita Mountains of Arizona, our group spent part of one afternoon sitting on a bench watching a row of seven hummingbird feeders in hopes of seeing a rare White-eared Hummingbird. So many territorial hummingbirds zip about at this amazing location that we feared the white-ear would be chased off seconds after it appeared. The moment we arrived, our leader pointed out each feeder and worked out a numbering system that we

**Where is that bird?**
Right over there. In the top of the tree. Not that tree. Too bad, you missed it.

83

**Why did the dinosaur cross the road?**

There weren't any chickens back then.

all understood. When the bird finally came, the woman who noticed it simply yelled out, "It's at number three!" and everyone found it instantly.

When looking at hawks or other migrating birds in the sky, clouds can be helpful. "It's in the center of the big cumulus cloud blocking the sun" is precise. But beware of "It's in the cloud that looks like a bunny." Soon everyone's attention will be directed to the shapes of clouds. Once at Hawk Ridge I heard this conversation: "It's in the cloud shaped like an armadillo." "No—that one's shaped like a cheeseburger." "No way—it's a stegosaurus!"

Night birds can be easily pointed out (if they're actually found, which is a different story) with flashlights or a spotlight. Before using spotlights, make sure they're legal in your state. Some states prohibit their night use outdoors to prevent the poaching of deer. ("Shining" deer roots them to the ground, making them easy targets.)

**What to do when you can't find a single bird**

Occasionally, despite all your planning and preparation, birds may simply be nowhere to be found on the day of your trip. Here's where a little ingenuity and humor on your part can save the day. I spend my life collecting interesting facts about birds that I can use to fill quiet, even desperate moments on field trips with adults as well as children. Learn about a few plants or nonavian animals for those times when birds seem invisible. Looking at cloud shapes and types, smelling the air, feeling and making tracings of tree bark patterns, listing all the sounds you can hear—these are all activities that can fill a low spot in the birding. This is an excellent time to pull Ogden Nash poems and bird jokes out of your memory. I also direct bored kids to look for other kinds of birds, from roosters on weather vanes to plastic lawn flamingos. A creative group can bring this to amazing heights of silliness. One frozen day in northern Minnesota, I took a group of Boy Scouts who were working on their Bird Study Merit Badge out with my Christmas Bird Count group. When birds were hard to find, we discovered new species, like the "Great Northern Shoveler," making its familiar scraping sounds. One boy pulled out his Scout knife and showed us a Burrowing Awl, so I pulled from my wallet a receipt for some silverware I'd just bought, marked it up with my red pen, and called it a "Roseate Spoon Bill."

**Why did the rooster cross the road?**

To meet the chicken.

**Why did the journalist write about the chicken crossing the road?**

To win the pullet surprise.

billing

preening

tail drag

driving

bow

nodding

wing clap

# 6

## LEARNING ABOUT BIRD BEHAVIOR

The beauty of birds captures our eyes, and the intensity and magic of their lives—gravity-defying flight, ethereal songs, exquisitely woven nests, tender, raucous, or downright silly nuptial displays—holds us under their spell. Birds perform feats mere humans can only dream of: A Peregrine Falcon hurls through the sky, tracking and intercepting a duck or shorebird that itself is erratically wheeling about, and strikes the victim so precisely with its talons that its own fragile wings and body aren't injured in the collision—all while flying 112 miles per hour. A three-month-old Ruby-throated Hummingbird, without any adult assistance or guidance, migrates from the northeastern United States all the way to the Texas coast, and then heads out over the Gulf of Mexico to fly nonstop over water a minimum of 620 miles to the Yucatan Peninsula. This bird is so tiny that you could mail ten with a single stamp, yet it performs this remarkable feat during hurricane season.

The more we know about a bird's life, the more interesting that bird becomes and the more easily we remember it. High school and college biology students often feel overwhelmed studying bazillions of unicellular and simple multicellular invertebrates, not because the students are unmotivated or stupid but because these microscopic critters don't *do* much of anything. The amoeba and hydra are

**Light as a feather**
A Ruby-throated
Hummingbird weighs
about one tenth of an
ounce—so little that you
could mail ten with a single
stamp. They prefer air mail.

the only two microscopic animals I remember clearly from college biology because these were the two that actually did things I could see and understand. Amoebas eat by engulfing their food, ultimately becoming one with their meals. As they grow and reach a certain size, they reproduce by splitting in two. Hydras hold prey as large as baby fish within grasping tentacles. These seemed to me exciting undertakings; other microscopic creatures just sat there under my microscope, little more than an odd assortment of physical characteristics to be keyed out and memorized for a test.

Listen to a three- or four-year-old talk about dinosaurs. You won't hear about physical characteristics except those associated with action, such as terrible claws and six-inch-long teeth. Dinosaur names evoke action, too. *Brontosaurus* means "thunder lizard," and most small children are happy to stomp around the living room pretending to be one. Birds are a lot more like dinosaurs than paramecia, and learning about their fun behaviors will help kids remember them in just the ways that they remember dinosaurs.

Studying behavior is worthwhile as more than just an identification tool. Charles Darwin's Galapagos Island studies of finch beaks and how they related to feeding behavior led to his formulation of the theory of evolution. Niko Tinbergen and Konrad Lorenz were both awarded Nobel prizes for discoveries about animal communication that were in part elucidated by their studies of avian displays. The more we understand about how birds live, the more they stimulate our minds.

Watching bird behavior may also nourish our hearts and souls. A robin outside our kitchen window, sitting tight on her eggs during a thunderstorm, teaches us something of steadfastness, devotion, and patience. A kingbird attacking a crow, hawk, or eagle demonstrates the meaning of courage and feistiness. A cardinal attacking its own image in our window as if battling a territorial intruder teaches about stubbornness and the inability to distinguish form from substance.

## Just the facts, ma'am

People have attributed human qualities to birds since earliest times. But one of the most important lessons a child should take from studying bird behavior is how to observe actions objectively. A fanciful child watching a robin on the front lawn might write, "The hungry robin ran eagerly on the lawn, stopped to listen for a worm, and when it heard one got excited, reached into the grass, grabbed it, and flew away to eat in privacy." A child trying to be more scientific might counter, "The robin ran five steps on the lawn, stopped, cocked its head for eight seconds, and pulled a worm out of the soil. I'm not sure if it knew where the worm was by seeing it, hearing it, or feeling the worm's vibrations with its feet. It carried the worm in its beak to the maple tree where its nest was, but the leaves were too thick for me to see whether it ate the worm itself or fed it to its mate or babies."

Gradually, as children study birds, they learn that bird behaviors and qualities are uniquely avian, not human, and that bird emotions are impossible for us to understand. *Anthropomorphizing* means attributing human characteristics to animals, which is unscientific. How can we say for sure that a singing bird is happy, rather than simply acting on an instinctive impulse that was triggered by an environmental or physiological factor?

However, it is equally unscientific to say that a singing bird is *not* happy, since we can't know for sure that birds don't feel the same happiness we do when we burst into song. We humans share much of our anatomy, physiology, and even biochemistry with birds, which are, after all, warm-blooded vertebrates with highly-developed senses and complex behaviors. We would have to sever all ties to our own natural heritage to ignore the many qualities, and perhaps emotions, that we have

**Kids can learn how to think about birds**

- poetically
- imaginatively
- objectively
- analytically
- artistically

**Head vs. heart**

A wild Pine Grosbeak and Ruby- and Golden-crowned Kinglets have on different occasions alighted on my hand when I was birding alone. The tiny ornithologist in my brain won't let me even speculate about why these birds came to me or looked into my eyes, but my heart can feel a reason.

in common with birds. People who set humans completely apart from animals, claiming it's impossible for animals to share human qualities or emotions, are perhaps guilty of "anthropocentrism," as untestable and thus as unscientific as anthropomorphism.

Our aim with children should be to encourage them to develop the objective skills necessary to look at things scientifically while keeping an open heart about mysteries that are in the realm of poetry and art. Once I came upon a fledgling Blue Jay in a park. I watched it hop on a playground slide, scoot up as high as it could get, and then slide back down. It did this seven or eight times while I watched and was still at it when I left. Most ethologists, the scientists who study animal behavior, agree that intelligent animals, such as jays and crows, really do play, perhaps to refine skills that may be useful for finding food or eluding predators. In the case of that baby Blue Jay, I prefer Mark Twain's explanation. He wrote, "It ain't no use to tell me a blue-jay hasn't got a sense of humor, because I know better."

There are so many kinds of bird behaviors and so many differences among species that ornithologists who spend a lifetime studying birds still feel humbled by how much they don't know. This chapter will barely scratch the surface of bird behavior and how to study it.

## A few principles of bird behavior

My friend Karen and I had babies within a couple of months of each other. We could tell Britta and Joey apart by their appearances, never mixing them up. We sometimes put them down together for naps while we visited together. The moment either of them woke up, we knew by the sound of the cry which baby was awake. But if we detected a suspicious odor, we had to actually peek into the diapers to tell which baby needed a change. Both babies felt pretty much the same to me, and I can't remember tasting either one. We humans may have five senses, but sight and hearing are the ones we most rely upon to learn about our environment and to recognize one another.

Birds, like us, depend primarily on their senses of sight and hearing—that's why the most noticeable things about them are their colors and songs. They communicate with one another using visual displays and vocalizations—pretty much like people. Avian communication is used to identify individuals, signal an intention to attack or escape, tell one another where they are, protect or take over a territory, indicate a desire to mate, or simply ask somebody to come play. Birds may also intentionally bluff or even deceive one another.

Ducklings open their eyes soon after hatching and can walk around as soon as their feathers dry. They recognize as "mother" the first thing they see moving and follow wherever she leads. This process is called *imprinting*, and it happens most dramatically in those birds, like ducks and chickens, that leave the nest right after hatching (*precocial* young). Wood Ducks nest in cavities high in trees. After the babies hatch and dry off, the mother sits on the forest floor beneath the nest and calls to them. One by one the babies respond to her calls by jumping out of the nest and falling to the ground—usually a thirty to fifty foot drop, comparable to jumping off the roof of a four-story building. The babies respond entirely from instinct. Mother ducks do not put food in their babies mouths—they lead them to food and the babies eat it themselves, again by instinct.

Baby songbirds just out of the egg are helpless, *altricial* young. They quietly nestle together until they feel a movement on the nest—then they pop up like little jack-in-the-boxes with their colorful mouths wide open. Parent songbirds must put food directly into their mouths because the babies can't feed themselves at all. As soon as a baby songbird swallows food, it immediately has to go to the bathroom—this timing is important so the parent will still be there to clean up the mess. An instinct tells the baby to back up to the edge of

**"Cheep talk"**

Birds begin communicating with one another while they're still in the egg. Baby ducks make little peeping sounds beginning a day or two before they hatch—these sounds help them to synchronize hatching so they'll be ready to leave the nest at the same time.

**Diaper disposal**
Grackles seem always to choose a swimming pool or bird bath to dispose of their babies' droppings.

the nest, and plop! Because baby songbird poop is encased in a strong membrane, the parent can pick it up without puncturing it and dump it someplace else. All a newly-hatched songbird knows how to do is eat and poop.

As birds grow, they develop more and more behaviors, some instinctive, some learned, and some a fascinating combination of the two. The first time a baby Blue Jay tastes an ant, it spits it out—ants are laced with formic acid, giving them a bitter taste. But then the Blue Jay rubs its tongue against the roof of its mouth and suddenly picks up the ant again—not to eat, but to rub on its feathers. This "anting" behavior coats the feathers with that bitter acid, which may serve as an insecticide. Baby Blue Jays don't learn this—it's completely instinctive. The behavior is apparently "released" by the bitter taste of the ant—some birds rub other bitter things on their feathers, too.

I have a license to keep a Blue Jay named Sneakers to use in educational programs. She plays with my children's Hot Wheels—little metal cars that go really fast on a smooth surface. When we line up the cars on the dining room table, she pushes them off one by one, and with each push she runs to the edge of the table to watch the car crash to the floor. When she's knocked all the cars down, she squawks until we line them up again. Playing with Hot Wheels is presumably not an instinctive behavior.

## Migration is a combination of learning and instinct

Canada Geese learn their migratory path and resting places from their parents. In autumn, Blue Jays gather in flocks to feed, young birds still learning from adults and one another, but parents often stay behind as young birds forge southward. Hummingbird adults leave days or even weeks ahead of their young, trusting that the map and compass inside their babies' brains will be enough to keep them on course.

Songbirds navigate by the stars. Young birds apparently spend part of their summer nights looking at the sky. Over time, they notice that all but one of the stars seem to move, revolving slowly around the one fixed star in the sky, Polaris. Come fall, these birds know which way to fly, thanks to this celestial compass. Scientists figured this out by raising birds in planetariums, where they could change the star patterns projected onto the circular walls. Using a special coating of dust on the floor to count bird tracks in each direction, or using special perches that recorded a signal whenever a bird landed on them, they could test which directions birds preferred. When they rotated the stars around Betelgeuse in autumn, birds gathered on the side opposite Betelgeuse ("south"). In spring, they gathered on the side toward Betelgeuse ("north").

On cloudy nights when stars are hard to see or even invisible, birds sometimes gravitate to the artificial lights on buildings and radio transmission towers. They mill about, bonking into the structure and one another. During the night of September 18, 1963, Dr. Charles Kemper and a university graduate student picked up 5,595 dead birds under a single television tower in Eau Claire, Wisconsin. The next night they picked up 4,600, bringing the two-night total of dead birds at a single tower to 10,195—and they probably missed well over half the birds! The powerful instinct to move toward stars in the night sky may be a fatal attraction in our lit-up modern world.

Ornithologists have also found traces of an iron metal called magnetite in the brains of birds. Pigeons apparently use both geomagnetism and the sun's position in the sky for homing. When ornithologists put little magnetic helmets on them, the pigeons got lost unless the sun was out. When the pigeons wore little nonmagnetic helmets of the same size and weight, they got home whether it was cloudy or not.

## Learning how to sing

The songs of birds, usually given only by males, are also a product of both instinct and learning. If a Song Sparrow egg is incubated in captivity so that the baby never hears his father or any other Song Sparrow, he will still sing a recognizable song when he grows up, but it won't be as complex as it would have been had he heard his father sing even one time. The first time a baby songbird hears the song of its own species, its heart beats faster. Even though it won't sing a note for many months, this early learning period is obviously very important.

Mockingbirds incorporate into their songs all kinds of sounds, from screeching tires to children playing. Females seem to prefer males who make the greatest variety of imitations, perhaps because the more sounds they make, the more life experiences they have successfully survived and the more likely they are to successfully deal with any difficulties that may arise during the coming breeding season.

True songs serve both to defend a territory and to attract a mate, though the relative importance of these purposes differs among species. Robins sing long after they're paired, working hard throughout the summer to keep other males off their territories, yet Boreal Owls, as soon as they've attracted a mate, shut up for the season—singing apparently puts them in too much danger from Barred and Great Horned Owls.

Besides the song, both male and female birds make many other sounds, usually referred to as call notes. Some bird recordings include a variety of *call notes* as well as songs and even provide explanations of the contexts in which they are given. (See chapter 2 for more information about recordings.) Sneakers, my Blue Jay, can say "Hi!" and "C'mon." She seems to do most of her talking when I'm out of sight, perhaps because she's calling to me and perhaps because when she can't hear me, she at least wants to hear something that sounds like me.

### Raising babies

The many behaviors involved in nest-building and raising young are mainly instinctive, but they improve with experience. Cedar Waxwings select the oldest mates they can attract because over time older birds have learned many important things that improve their babies' chances of survival. (They recognize older birds by the number of red, waxy tips on secondary wing feathers.) But some parental instincts are so strong, they seem to defy the benefits of learning. For example, adult songbirds have a powerful instinct to stuff food into their babies' mouths. This instinct is partly triggered by the bright color and wide shape of baby songbird mouths. Small songbirds often feed a baby cowbird even as their own young starve because the cowbird has a bigger, more conspicuous mouth that elicits a powerful feeding response.

## Finding bird behaviors to study

Being in the right place at the right time to see birds do interesting things certainly involves luck, but it's mostly a matter of spending time outside paying attention. One or two children can creep about, easily sneaking up on birds to observe many moments in their private lives. With large groups of children, behavior watches are easiest, most fun, and most instructive when we find places with conspicuous birds allowing us to observe closely without intruding on them, causing them to either fly away or change the behaviors we want to see. The more you learn about local birding opportunities, the easier it will be to know where to take kids.

Some birds are more visible and more tolerant of disturbances than others. A few species that offer good opportunities for large or small groups to observe them include neighborhood pigeons; Canada Geese in local parks; loons, grebes, and waterfowl in lakes and ponds, especially in spring when they're courting; Red-winged Blackbirds on territory in cattail marshes in spring; seabird colonies (if you happen to have an ocean handy); herons and egrets at marshes and heronries; bluebirds, Purple Martins, or Tree Swallows at nest boxes; other swallows in nesting colonies; eagles at rivers and dams in winter;

**Bird adopts fish?**

Once, in North Carolina, a cardinal who apparently lost his young spent several days delivering mouthfuls of worms and bugs to goldfish in a garden pool! The goldfish mouths were similar in color and size to baby cardinal mouths.

**Owl moon**

Jane Yolen's Caldecott award-winning book *Owl Moon* is about a father and daughter's magical night in search of an owl.

and songbirds at feeders. Find a vantage point where everyone can sit down comfortably while watching the action.

Figuring out territorial boundaries, finding nests, and watching courtship displays are all richly rewarding studies, but they are usually more successful when children work alone or in pairs than when they're in large groups. One or two children can watch an oriole nest without disturbing the birds unlike a whole mob of kids. A large group of kids would be hard to keep track of in semidarkness watching an April woodcock skydance or moving about at night listening for owls, but one or two children with an adult could have a magical time. On a walk along a quiet woodland path, two or three people can sit down to watch a catbird skulking in shrubbery or a group of small birds bombarding a Blue Jay approaching a nest without affecting the behaviors as much as a class of thirty would do. But even so, don't underestimate the ability of a whole class to be absolutely silent when called upon in a special situation.

Some children will be less interested in spending long periods of time studying bird behavior than others. Making opportunities for long-term studies is more within the realm of parents and grandparents than of classroom teachers, but teachers are often the ones who plant the seeds that inspire children to study bird behavior on their own.

**What to look for**

Our task is to help children develop both observation skills and the ability to separate actions into individual components. It's a good idea to begin a study of bird behavior with one or two species chosen from a Stokes' behavior guide (see Appendix III). Under the Canada Goose entry, the guide provides seven drawings of goose postures, and behaviors and descriptions of two others; it also describes four calls and their meanings. The simple drawings are easy for even preschoolers to understand, and older children (and adults) will appreciate the storehouse of information about how birds go about their daily lives. To prepare for a class trip to observe geese in a local park, children might read about the displays and copy or trace the drawings into their field notebooks. Then, when they arrive at the park, they will have some idea of what to watch for. This will make the trip more interesting and fun than if they came upon geese without any knowledge of what their behaviors meant.

The behavior accounts in the Stokes' guides are simplified, offering no explanation of some behaviors that observant children may see, but overall they include the most common actions and postures that we are likely to see. One great advantage to this series is that every description is written using scientific terms. Children have vivid imaginations and automatically place value judgements and interpretations on bird behaviors—these books will help them think more scientifically. Once they've used these guides to interpret some behaviors, they will have the skills to start interpreting other bird behaviors. The Cornell Laboratory of Ornithology's Project PigeonWatch is another perfect introduction to behavior watching (see Chapter 2).

To study nesting or territorial behavior of birds that live in your yard or on school grounds, you might set up a tent or a photographer's portable observation blind near a known nesting spot. Or try draping a sheet or blanket with a small peep hole over a crouching child or two. Cars and school buses also make effective observation blinds. Two or three quiet people in a canoe or kayak can sneak up on water and marsh birds. Constructing a bird feeder or robin nest platform near a window, establishing a swallow or bluebird trail near school or home, or just setting out a wren house may provide matchless opportunities for intimate study of birds feeding, defending territory, courting, and raising their babies.

Don't forget to study the behavior of indoor birds, too. Because they breed so readily in captivity, zebra finches offer

**Focus on behaviors**

When beginning a study of any bird, give specific behaviors to watch for such as:

- diving
- striking at fish
- feeding babies
- head bobbing
- displaying wing patterns
- scratching
- singing

Use stopwatches to figure out the number of actions per minute. Encourage the children to concentrate on the task at hand, but be flexible. Just because they're assigned to count red-wing epaulet displays doesn't mean they can't take time out to watch an Osprey catch a fish.

**Learning on their own**

Answers to some tricky questions are available in good bird books, but many questions may incubate in children's minds until they figure out ways of learning the answers on their own. Thus are ornithologists born.

opportunities for a wide range of behavior and natural history study, but canaries, budgies, and cockatiels also do interesting things that children will enjoy defining and interpreting.

Children will come up with bazillions of questions about what they are seeing. Some answers will be easy for them to figure out for themselves. Which birds hop, which walk, and which do both? To preen their heads, which birds use direct head-scratching (lifting their foot to their head, leaving their wing closed) and which use indirect head-scratching (opening their wing and lifting their foot behind and over the extending wing)? Do robins sing with their mouths open or closed? Do they breathe as they sing?

Watching nesting birds, children may wonder whether both parents or just the mother incubates the eggs. If the birds are orioles or cardinals, the answer is easy to see because the male and female birds look very different. But if the birds are Blue Jays or Chipping Sparrows, because males and females look identical, the only way to learn the answer, unless one bird has an obvious abnormality, is to band or color-mark individuals. Unfortunately, these studies can be done legally only by licensed researchers.

## A seasonal guide to bird behavior

Natural cycles drive bird behavior, and behavior-study activities are best planned with the seasons of the year in mind. Snow doesn't instantly melt and tropical migrants magically reappear on March 21. In early July, when late migrants such as cuckoos are just starting to nest in the northern tier of states, the earliest migrants from the far north, the shorebirds, are already heading south. And fall migration may continue into the sledding season. So ornithologists who organize field data divide the year differently than astronomers do. *Audubon Field Notes*, a technical journal published by the National Audubon Society, defines autumn as the time from August 1 to November 30, winter from December 1 to February 28, spring from

March 1 to May 31, and summer from June 1 to July 31. It's fun and instructive to keep a phenology record, keeping track of when birds arrive and depart and the dates from year to year when they first sing, nest, and fledge young.

## Autumn

Wild bird activities in autumn are driven by the coming winter, but not directly because of cold temperatures. Birds are surprisingly hardy and able to withstand temperature extremes—that's the whole point of being warm-blooded and having thick down insulation. But those birds adapted to catching cold-blooded animals or feeding on aquatic plants or animals will starve if they remain north when subfreezing temperatures eliminate their food supplies or hide them under snow and ice. In some areas of the country, such as the southwestern desert and the California coast, rainfall patterns may affect plants and animals more than temperature extremes, so avian seasonal cycles vary geographically.

To cope with seasonal changes of any kind, many birds simply adjust their diets to take advantage of whatever food resource is most available. Chickadees, which eat many tiny caterpillars and other moving insects in warm months, turn to seeds and to eggs and pupae hidden in tree crevices during winter. Some Common Poorwills actually hibernate during winter. But most birds fly from place to place seasonally to find food. Many of the birds we see in late summer and fall are migrants.

Birds have internal rhythms that help them prepare for seasonal events. Days grow shorter beginning on the summer solstice, and after the autumn equinox nights grow increasingly longer than days. Birds sense these changes, and their bodies adjust in several ways. After the breeding season, sex organs shrink in most adult birds and don't develop at all in young birds—after all, sex organs are nothing but excess baggage to lug around if birds aren't breeding anyway.

**Bird photography**

Many kids bring along a camera on bird walks and take lots of pictures of distant birds. They are often disappointed when the film comes back and their birds are nothing but specks.

Professional bird photographers usually use single lens reflex cameras with a long telephoto lens—rather pricey for a little kid. Most family cameras can be set on a tripod near a nest or feeder. The budding photographers can hide under a blanket or at some distance, holding onto an inexpensive but long cable release to take the picture when the bird returns.

To prepare for the journey, migratory birds gorge themselves, producing special fat deposits which they "burn up" during migration. They become restless at night and develop an urge to head south. (In spring the shorter nights will send them the opposite direction.)

Many birds time their fall movement to coincide with abundant food to fuel the flight. Hundreds of American Kestrels move along the north shore of Lake Superior in August and September on days when swarms of dragonflies are also moving. Sharp-shinned Hawks and Merlins, who eat little birds, migrate during the peak of songbird migration. Cedar Waxwings and robins harvest late summer's ripening berries. Ruby-throated Hummingbirds seem to follow the jewelweed blossom "crop." Cold days slow down or kill flying insects, and so migrants that depend on them, such as nighthawks and swallows, must leave before the first killing frost. The last swallow to leave the north, the Tree Swallow, is capable of eating and digesting berries when insects aren't available.

Many warblers leave their northeastern U.S. breeding grounds in August. One that lingers well into October, the Yellow-rumped Warbler, has longer intestines than other warblers and produces an enzyme that breaks down wax, allowing it to digest plant as well as insect matter—it's especially adapted for eating wax myrtle berries. Many yellow-rumps remain in the central and southern states rather than going all the way to the tropics as their relatives do.

## Studying behavior in fall

Migration can't be understood from one spot. When people lived in small villages where they remained their whole lifetimes, they noticed that birds appeared and disappeared seasonally, but they lacked the geographic scope to figure out migration. It wasn't until explorers traveled long distances that they realized that birds don't bury themselves under mud or fly to the moon for the winter.

Not all birds feed and migrate at the same time. Broad-winged Hawks depend on updrafts and thermal air currents to carry them aloft. They're headed for Central and South America, but that's an awfully long distance to flap their long, wide wings, so they conserve energy by migrating mostly when rising air currents are available. They gather in swirling groups called kettles, all circling upward as far as air currents will carry them and then streaming out in a long band, hardly flapping their wings at all. On days when migrating conditions are perfect, they may travel long distances without eating. At the Hawk Ridge Nature Reserve banding station, on those days when the broad-wing count exceeds 10,000, other hawks are trapped and banded by the dozens or hundreds, but broad-wings are too busy flying high to notice the bait at all.

Flyways where hawks or waterfowl gather are excellent places for children to study migration behavior in fall. Hummingbirds and some songbirds, such as kingbirds, swallows, jays, robins, and blackbirds, migrate by day and may be observed along shorelines and ridges, but their movements are not nearly as conspicuous as those of larger birds.

To actually observe nocturnal migration, some people focus a spotting scope on the moon and watch birds winging past—a fun activity for parents, scout leaders, and other adults who are with children at nighttime. When the birds aren't flying, you can check out those moon craters.

Watching migrants by day or night, most birders focus on identification. Children can keep a count of the birds seen during a specified period and then make simple bar graphs to compare the numbers of each species seen, or they can keep track hour by hour to see if numbers of some species increase as numbers of others decrease. But it's more fun to see and graph flying behaviors.

Some hawks hunt as they migrate—American Kestrels often dart at dragonflies, and Merlins dart at small birds. When

**Fall bird watching**

In autumn, the simplest behaviors for children to observe are feeding, flocking, and migrating. Sometimes all three behaviors can be seen simultaneously—when Common Nighthawks are on the move in August and early September, huge numbers dart through the skies catching bugs as they head toward South America.

101

### do they fly?

may wonder how high birds fly. Design an experiment at a migration observation point using a long kite string tied to a helium balloon. Mark the string with ink every meter, or yard, to keep track of length. Someone may draw a bird on the balloon, making it about the size of a Sharp-shinned Hawk, and then the class can compare its size at given heights with the size of flying sharpies. Sometimes children may be able to see directly how many birds are flying above and how many below the balloon.

For reference; according to Clay Sutton and Patricia Taylor Sutton in *How to Spot Hawks and Eagles*, Broad-winged Hawks disappear to the naked eye at about 2,100 feet in a cloudless sky; the smaller Sharp-shinned Hawk disappears at about 1,650 feet.

Sharp-shinned Hawks are hunting, they fly low over the trees, flapping several times and then soaring for two or three seconds. When they're strictly migrating (presumably because they have a full stomach), they fly high, soaring for long periods with wings and tail spread wide. Using a stopwatch, children can see how much time various birds spend flapping as opposed to gliding or soaring. How many times per minute do various hawks flap their wings?

Nocturnal migrants spend much of their day feeding. Warblers, vireos, and kinglets move about in mixed flocks, often joining with local chickadees, and spend autumn days feeding, moving generally south as they search for insects. They especially abound near lakes and streams where insects swarm. Warblers are so tiny and active that they're hard to keep track of, but the more time children spend watching them at a good spot, the more they will notice. Yellow-rumped Warblers and American Redstarts flutter out over water to catch insects on the wing; Palm Warblers delicately wag their tails while sitting on the ground; and Black-and-white Warblers creep about tree trunks like nuthatches. Firsthand observations like these will enrich any child's field notebook.

## ESPECIALLY FOR GROUPS

To observe autumn feeding behaviors with large groups of children, gather at a feeding station or at a mountain ash or crab apple tree. Observe how far apart different birds sit. Chickadees grab a seed and fly off, keeping quite a distance from one another, while sparrows, grosbeaks, and finches often sit shoulder to shoulder. Some of these birds bicker and fight when they're too crowded. How much personal territory does each species maintain? Blue Jays living in the vicinity of a feeder usually stuff their throat pouches with seeds and fly off to hide or eat them elsewhere—they use feeders as grocery stores. Jays traveling through an area eat their seeds one by one, using the feeder as a restaurant. When Blue Jays are feeding in a group, they keep their crests lowered—a signal that they will not treat one another aggressively. Hummingbirds seldom cooperate like that—often one will chase another away from a sugar water feeder even when three or more drinking ports are available. How do the robins eating in fruit trees get along?

After a behavior-watching session, it's both fun and worthwhile for kids and grown-ups to discuss their observations. Sometimes several children will have noticed the same activity, and they may draw conclusions or generalizations. Sometimes two children may have seen things that seem inconsistent— one may watch Blue Jays peacefully eating together while another spots a Blue Jay squawking or pecking at another. Little by little, on their own the children will notice more about the lives of birds, thanks to these discussions.

If your class or family is compiling a personal field guide with pictures of the various birds you've seen together, include behavior information as well as identification marks. If the bird visits your feeding station, list the foods it takes. Does it come alone or in a flock? What calls does it make? The more observations you include, the more interesting and useful this book will be. Make sure to include dramatic scenes—if you see a shrike attacking a chickadee, mention it on both the shrike and chickadee pages.

## Winter

Migration continues throughout winter. Although neotropical migrants (birds that migrate to the New World tropics) are gone, birds from the far north may move south and then north again as the season progresses. During some winters, northern finches or owls may appear in central and even southern states.

Winter birds spend the majority of their time sleeping, as nights are longer than days. Finding sleeping birds is difficult at best, and in winter it's not only rude to disturb them, it can also endanger their lives. Some children have the curiosity and patience to follow backyard birds to night roost sites just to figure out where they go.

The most easily observed winter bird activity is eating. To survive the coldest nights, birds must have food, which they metabolize, or convert to usable energy, to heat their bodies. The easiest place to observe a variety of feeding birds is at feeders. Children might study which kinds of food each bird eats and the techniques different species use to eat the same thing. For example, birds eat sunflower seeds in various ways. Mourning Doves swallow the whole seed, shell and all, leaving it to their gizzard to grind it open. Jays and chickadees hold a single sunflower seed in their feet—jays hack the shell off and eat the sunflower heart in one or two gulps while chickadees chip a hole into the seed shell and break off tiny pieces of the heart one by one. Finches wedge seeds into internal ridges of their mouth as they crack them open against their sharp beak edge using powerful jaw muscles. Then their muscular tongue extracts the heart and spits out the shell.

Children may experiment with food preferences at feeders. Patient kids may try to teach birds to take seeds from their hands. On warmer days, birds sip water from melting icicles or bathe beneath them. House Sparrows sometimes take snow baths. Offer a bowl of water outside a window and see if birds come.

Even in the dead of winter, birds don't live by food and water alone—they occasionally nap. A large group of children searching for roosting chickadees or finches has a low probability of success, but patient, observant children may come upon them now and again. Some resting birds are easy to spot. Pigeons roost on window ledges and other structures. Starlings sit on chimneys, warming their little fannies. Mourning Doves often bide their time on a sheltered, sunny branch. Juncoes seek shelter from bitterly cold winds by sitting near the trunks of coniferous trees, getting warmth in a shaft of sunlight. On days when temperatures plummet well below zero, House Sparrows often watch and listen, waiting for people to park their cars and shut the engines off. Sometimes, before a person even slams the car door, sparrows dart under the hood to soak up engine warmth. They fly out when the engine cools down.

As the season progresses and days grow longer, birds spend more and more time on activities other than feeding and roosting. Woodpeckers start drumming and chickadees sing more and more. Owls nest in the middle of winter—beginning in February or March even in the northernmost states. A phenology chart gets wonderfully exciting as kids discover signs of spring.

## Spring

Lengthening days after the winter solstice cause increases in blood hormone levels. As in the fall, changing hormone levels cause birds to put on fat deposits and grow restless to migrate. But spring migration is impelled by more than just the need to find food. Under the influence of surging hormones, avian sex organs swell. Suddenly male birds urgently need to find and defend a territory, sing, and attract a mate. Females urgently need to lay eggs, and they and the males of some species urgently need to build a nest and incubate and feed young. So while fall migration is a fairly leisurely occurrence for many species, spring migration moves fast and furious.

Many migrants that winter in the central and southern states respond to weather patterns. For example, Canada Geese and robins migrate behind the 37 degree isotherm, following the spring thaw. From year to year, the first date that these migrants appear may vary by weeks. Tropical migrants usually time their flights by day length, and so they arrive close to the same date each year. But no birds arrive according to a precise schedule.

**Swallows of Capistrano**

The Cliff Swallows that nest at the mission at San Juan Capistrano no longer appear as regularly as they once did because development along the California coast has reduced their population.

The reason Cliff Swallows are never seen at the mission at San Juan Capistrano until St. Joseph's feast day on March 19 is simply because people keep their eyes averted until that day.

## Studying behavior in spring

In early spring, before migrants return, fewer birds are living in the United States than at any other time of year, yet this marks the beginning of the richest opportunities for bird-watching and study. Birds that have survived fall migration and the hard winter now wear their most conspicuous plumage and proclaim their territorial rights in full song. As migration proceeds, listening to bird songs, watching how different species weave their nests, seeing parent songbirds feed their babies, studying how different baby birds learn to fly—the possibilities for watching bird behavior become endless. Hiding in tents or portable observation blinds (or simply under a blanket) may allow close-up viewing.

Ducks, loons, and other water birds appear on ponds, streams, and lakes almost as soon as ice disappears. Ducks are courting, and males' display behaviors are fun and exciting to watch. Male grackles strut on front lawns, puffing out their feathers like adolescent boys showing off their muscles.

Take one or two children out on an April evening to see male woodcocks spiraling skyward in their nocturnal dance. Prepare the kids ahead of time by playing a recording of the performance. Woodcocks begin at dusk, making "peent" sounds on the ground. They may repeat their calls for many minutes before suddenly one takes off, spiraling up toward the clouds, its wings making a lovely chittering sound. When it reaches a height of about 300 feet, it makes liquid chirps almost like a canary and suddenly drops like a falling leaf, peenting when it reaches the ground. This lovely performance happens only in semidarkness when even the keenest-eyed children will miss much of it, but if the children know what is happening as they hear each sound, they're usually motivated enough to search the dark sky and will feel rewarded by even shadow-glimpses of these plump, endearing shorebirds. Recordings of woodcocks generally include an entire sky-dance cycle.

## Summer

Summer is an in-between time in the lives of children and the lives of birds. During summer vacation, when school-age children have their greatest opportunities to watch birds on their own, most birds are continuing the spring activities of breeding and nesting. By midsummer most are preparing for fall migration. In August, many birds depart, and migrants from farther north pass through. In most areas, no other season offers as many rich and varied opportunities for behavior study.

For children who still enjoy the luxury of summer vacation, this is a magical stretch of days when time piles up like billowy cumulus clouds. Encourage children to explore deeply the things they are interested in, including bird study. If they do it on their own, with little more than encouragement and a few useful tools from you, the ownership of their discoveries will be theirs alone. Feelings of pride and satisfaction from self-taught learning give young lives direction, passion, and meaning.

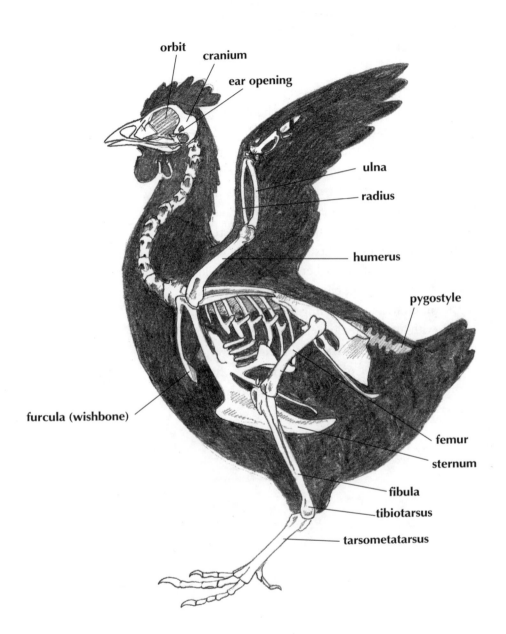

orbit

cranium

ear opening

ulna

radius

humerus

pygostyle

furcula (wishbone)

femur

sternum

fibula

tibiotarsus

tarsometatarsus

# 7

## LEARNING HOW BIRD BODIES WORK

Which came first—the chicken or the egg? Birds evolved from dinosaurs or similar reptiles, so the first bird obviously came from an egg, while the first egg must have been laid by something more primitive than a bird. In this chapter, we'll look at adult birds first and then at the eggs they produce. Whether covered by feathers or a shell, bird bodies and how they work fascinate children and adults.

Birds are designed for flight. Many bones are hollow, often filled with air sacs which not only decrease weight but also increase the amount of air a bird takes in and processes during each breath. The avian body is streamlined for flight. Food is ground by a gizzard near the bird's center of gravity rather than by heavy, forward-set teeth. Efficient circulatory and respiratory systems permit carefree aerial maneuvers at altitudes too high for mere humans to remain conscious without an oxygen tank.

**Children are empathetic**
Although live birds provide glimpses into the workings of their bodies, to fully see and understand how they work requires dead ones. Plucking feathers, examining bare skin, and looking at "innards" can be wonderfully interesting and even fun. But dead birds conjure up sad and fearful emotions, too, and

**Supermarket birds**
A store-bought chicken or turkey can provide interesting lessons in avian biology.

**Don't overdo it!**
Although dissection projects are fascinating, showing many miracles of biology, too many dissections may desensitize children. Also, one or two dissections done as demonstrations with a lot of discussion and the children helping out may provide more valuable learning experiences for everyone than having each child do a dissection individually.

many children hate the very idea that an animal has to die just so they can study it. That's why people respond so enthusiastically to the frog-release scene in the movie *E.T.* It's ironic when a biology project intended to inspire appreciation of life requires the destruction of life.

When I was in fifth grade, my class was told to bring earthworms to school to dissect. I couldn't bring myself to single out a worm to die, even though I badly wanted to see how their bodies work. My teacher, Mr. Borkowski, told me he'd find me a worm "that's already dead." It took me years to realize how much empathy and compassion those simple words conveyed.

When I was a college student majoring in education, during my first opportunity to observe a classroom in action, I watched fifth-graders dissecting frogs. The teacher had arranged for a prominent professor to lead the activity, and he brought live frogs which he expected the children to kill by *pithing*—that is severing their spinal cord with a sharp probe. When I came onto the scene, one little boy was crying—it turned out he had frogs for pets. I couldn't imagine anyone but a tyrant forcing him to dissect one, much less to actually kill it, but his teacher not only insisted, she gripped his hand and forced the probe down into a live frog's spinal cord. She thought a sentimental attachment to frogs was incompatible with scientific inquiry.

If a pet or classroom bird dies, it's not a good idea to dissect it—the experience will be too sad for the children. Although I am both a bird rehabilitator and a researcher, I usually have no trouble dissecting nighthawks that have died under my care, but there have been two with whom I developed such a special bond that, when they died, we buried them in the backyard.

## So where do you get dead animals?
As a teacher, Brownie leader, and mom, I've dissected animals

with children from ages four through sixteen. We always plan the activity beginning with a discussion about how we feel about animals dying and us cutting into them. Every group with which I've done this has come to the same general consensus—they're unwilling or at least reluctant to dissect anything that died specifically for them, whether the animal arrived dead or not. This means I've never worked on frogs with kids.

Birds that have been considered acceptable by at least some of my classes include chickens and turkeys from local poultry farms and birds killed by cats or by flying into picture windows. Friends or relatives who hunt game birds may provide dissecting opportunities. Hunters usually eat their game but are often happy to provide wings, feet, and other interesting parts for study. A single duck or pheasant wing can provide an incredible assortment of beautiful and interesting feathers.

My students were happiest dissecting road kills, especially after discussing what happens when dead animals are left on roads to attract scavengers, which may in turn be killed. The problem with road kills is that some wild animals harbor parasites or diseases—make sure that the animal looks healthy (well, except for being dead). Most avian lice and mites "jump ship" as soon as a bird's body cools, so they're virtually never a problem, but road kills may be unpleasant to work with unless they're very fresh. One time a student's mom froze a dead Indigo Bunting for us without realizing that maggots had already hatched on it. Fortunately, freezing killed them, and they dropped off the specimen like grains of rice, but I prefer not to deal with maggots, even dead ones.

Before beginning a dissection, talk with children about the possibility of contacting germs, reminding them that after they've touched an animal, they mustn't put their fingers by their faces until they've washed their hands with soap. Mammals harbor more diseases that humans can catch than birds do—in the many years I've rehabilitated wild birds, including sick ones, in my house, my children have never gotten sick

**Problems with pigeons**

Pigeons from biological supply houses may come injected with latex to demonstrate fine details of the circulatory system that can't be seen in fresh or frozen birds. These preserved specimens were healthy when killed, so using them may violate some children's and adults' sensibilities. If you do work with them, make sure to wear rubber gloves— although almost all the formalin has been washed away on properly prepared specimens, traces do remain. Without rubber gloves, fingers get wrinkled and rubbery. When I worked on a preserved pigeon, my fingers tingled for two days, and each time I washed my hands, I smelled formalin.

111

from one, and I have only once. Be prudent, but don't let worries keep you from offering a great learning experience.

Birds native to America are protected by law, so to legally possess or dissect those that have been found dead, you must have state and federal licenses, be working under the auspices of a licensed institution, or have taken a game bird legally with a hunting license. It's also illegal to possess the feathers of protected species, which include just about every native American bird. The Migratory Bird Act is a reasonable but broad law designed to protect wild birds. Most state and federal enforcement officers understand the law's intent and don't make it difficult for teachers to use already-dead birds for educational purposes. Starlings, House Sparrows, and Rock Doves are not protected by law and may be dissected without any legal implications at all.

When my students found dead birds, we called an especially helpful university museum curator. If he needed a good specimen for his collection, we examined its exterior body and then brought it to him to prepare professionally. If he didn't need a perfect representative of that species, he sometimes allowed us to stuff it as a study specimen for him. Our first efforts were hardly the best, but some of my fifth-graders gained more experience at study-skin preparation techniques than modern graduate-level university students usually get. Sometimes the curator had so many of a given species that he allowed us to dissect our specimen. (Dissecting pretty much demolishes a bird, making its skin worthless.) My students dissected or prepared skins of several songbirds, from warblers to crows, in our classroom, and my second-grade Brownies once dissected a Great Horned Owl on my dining room table.

ESPECIALLY FOR GROUPS

## Before you cut

Any time I've begun a dissection of any creature, I've started out by simply looking at the still-intact dead animal. Many kids think curiosity and sadness are incompatible. In my experience, tenderhearted children are reluctant to cut into road kills because they don't want to be hard and unfeeling, not because they lack interest or curiosity or because they think dissecting is wrong. Curious children, on the other hand, seem to believe that they mustn't show, or even feel, any sadness about the death. Regardless of interest, just about every kid new to dissecting will expect it to be at least a little gross. Because of this difficult ambivalence, and because some kids like to get a rise out of grown-ups or other kids, someone may giggle, act silly, or try to upset the others. Dissections will teach a lot more than biology when children are required to show absolute respect toward the animal and one another. This is such an unusual and fascinating activity that, when you set clear ground rules, even children who are capable of obnoxious behavior virtually always cooperate. In my classroom, the penalty for violating the rules was to be banished from the dissection entirely—any child who broke a rule would have to write a report about bird biology instead. Guess what? Not one kid ever broke the rules.

I never require participation in dissection projects. In my classroom, everyone was responsible for the information covered, but I provided interesting, easy-to-follow reference books and gave squeamish kids and conscientious objectors the option of studying the material on their own. Despite that option, not one student skipped an entire dissection. (A lot of kids did wince or even keep their eyes shut when we dissected an eyeball. That's the worst part for me, too.) When my Brownies dissected an owl, most of them were thrilled by the opportunity, but a couple chose to spend part of the time in another room. My daughter, Katie, has usually been fascinated by dissections I've done at home for my research on nighthawk physiology, but Joey and Tommy often prefer to leave the house for the duration.

**More problems
with pigeons**

The feathers of preserved specimens from biological supply houses are coated with preservatives, weighing them down and giving them a wet, bedraggled appearance that makes it difficult to observe the various feather types and colors. Also, the chemicals injected into preserved specimens may make relative weights of internal organs, especially the lungs, inaccurate.

If you choose not to do dissections with children, books and magazines can provide much of the same information. If you feel too squeamish, uninformed, or distressed to actually cut into a dead bird but don't mind handling it a bit, help children examine the outside for a fine introductory lesson in avian biology. This can be a planned activity or might simply happen when you come upon a dead bird on a walk to the grocery store.

---

### From the outside looking in

A simple dissection kit, available at most college bookstores as well as through biological and teaching supply catalogs (see Chapter 2 for sources), is very useful. Even if you're just going to examine the outside of a dead bird, the probe and forceps will be invaluable for holding feathers aside to allow viewing of hidden features such as ears, especially on small birds. It's a good idea to have some plastic drinking straws of various sizes, including tiny coffee stirrers, on hand for inflating air sacs. A scale or balance that can weigh things as small as a gram (or less) is very useful. Weigh your bird before starting, and also weigh some plastic bags. As you pluck feathers, put them in a bag—at the end, you may want to determine what fraction of the bird's weight was feathers.

When working on road kills and birds killed by cats or flying against windows, it's interesting to try to figure out the cause of death. During some of the years I taught, a show about a doctor of forensic medicine was on TV, and all the kids wanted to play "Quincy." You probably won't be absolutely sure, but sometimes a bruised liver, a puncture to the lungs, or black spinal fluid leaking out of the mouth will give a clue.

### In fine feather

The first thing we look at on a dead or living bird is its plumage. No creatures in the universe except birds have feathers—they are the single unique feature that defines Class Aves. Most ornithologists believe feathers originated for one of two purposes—either to provide insulation as birds became warm-blooded or to aid in flight. Feathers are outgrowths of the skin made mostly of beta keratin. This protein molecule is similar to the alpha keratin that produces our hair and fingernails.

Most feather colors are derived from pigments. If you grind up a red or a yellow feather, you'll end up with reddish or yellowish powder. But some feather colors are caused by light reflecting off a thin layer of cells on the surface, just like bubble colors. These are called *structural colors*. If you find a feather from a Blue Jay, notice how blue it is when light shines on it. Then hold it up so light shines through it. This exposes the feather's true pigment color—a dull brownish gray. All blue feathers are colored structurally. Iridescence is also structural. A yellow pigment blends with a blue structural color to produce green feathers.

Not all colors on birds come from their feathers. Some species, such as turkeys, cranes, and vultures, have brightly-colored patches of bare skin. Some male birds, such as Lesser and Greater Prairie-Chickens and Sharp-tailed and Sage Grouse, have colorful air sacs which they inflate during breeding displays.

When a child finds a feather outdoors, it's fun to guess what bird it came from and what kind of feather it is. Virtually every feather we find is a flight or a body feather. If it's considerably longer than it is wide and has a stiff shaft, it's probably a flight feather; if it's almost as wide as or wider than it is long, it's more likely to be a body feather. If a flight feather is very asymmetric, with one side noticeably wider than the other, it's probably from a wing. The thinner, stiffer side is usually the leading edge in flight, so you can even figure out whether it came from a left or right wing. Tail feathers are usually more symmetric and straighter than wing feathers. It's fun to look at

**How many feathers do birds have?**

The Smithsonian Institution initiated a feather-counting project in 1933. They didn't count the feathers from birds of every species, but some of their results were:

Tundra Swan 25,216

Bobolink 3,235

Ruby-crowned
  Kinglet 1,119

Ruby-throated
  Hummingbird 940

**Valuable insulation**

Down is the finest insulating material known. Eighty percent of all the down feathers that fill our jackets, pillows, and sleeping bags is imported from the goose and duck meat industries of China, Germany, and France. Eider down is the softest, most insulating, and most valuable down of all, costing hundreds of dollars per pound. It comes from eider nests on the frozen tundra. Female eiders tear this down from their bellies and breasts to line the nests, protecting eggs from the permafrost below. Laws in Canada, Greenland, and Iceland regulate collectors and limit how much down they can collect from each nest. An eider down collector named Hans was hired as a guide in Jules Verne's *Journey to the Center of the Earth.*

feathers under a magnifying glass or backwards binoculars to scrutinize their intricate structure.

Some feathers, such as those of Blue Jays and flickers, are easy to recognize; others are much trickier. Scientists can identify virtually all feathers under a microscope. The world's most noted authority on feather identification, Roxie Laybourne, works at the Smithsonian Institution in Washington, D.C. She can identify even charred and burned feathers from birds that were sucked into airplane engines. Feather identification once helped solve a murder—feathers embedded in a fatal wound were proven to have come from a pillow that the murderer used to muffle the sound of the gunshot.

Feathers grow out of little pimple-like structures on the skin called *papillae.* These bumps are easy to see on store-bought chickens and turkeys. The genes in the papillae determine what colors each feather will be. Papillae are arranged on the skin in a pattern—areas where feathers grow are called *feather tracts.* Naked areas of skin between the feather tracts are called *apteria.* Feathers are large enough to overlap, so apteria are only visible when birds are very young or after they are plucked. The base of each papilla is surrounded by ligaments which can move the feather, and birds can control the position of many of their feathers.

Ornithologists usually recognize six feather types, but the feathers we actually see on birds are almost all one type, called *contour feathers.* These feathers have a fairly stiff shaft or quill and two complete webs of barbs on each side (*vanes*); they get their name from the fact that they form the outline of the bird. Contour feathers include the outer body feathers and the flight feathers. In some species, especially birds like pheasants and grouse, body feathers are double, with a large outer feather and a smaller twin, called an *after-feather,* attached at the base.

Other types of feathers are *down feathers,* soft and fluffy insulating feathers growing close to the skin, which are usually gray or white; *semiplumes*, white with a stiff shaft and soft, downy vanes, which grow along the edges of the feather tracts; *filoplumes*, specialized, hairlike feathers which sense vibrations in the contour feathers and transmit the sensation to the skin; *bristles*, found almost exclusively on the head, especially near the mouth and nostrils, which probably serve protective and sensory purposes (for example, they help Whip-poor-wills detect contact with a flying insect and reorient their mouths to catch it); and *powder down*, continually growing feathers, which break down to a waxy powder—in herons and bitterns they soak up fish slime and oil, and in many other species they help waterproof and condition the feathers. Even a cursory examination of a dead bird's feathers will reveal flight and body feathers, down, and sometimes bristles by the mouth or nostrils. Looking more carefully, you may find some of the other feather types.

Look at the whole plumage as well as individual feathers. Birds that spend a lot of time in or near water often have plumage that feels waxy—the contour feathers on these birds hold water away from the bird's down feathers. It rolls away "like water off a duck's back." Owls have very soft, loose plumage. If your bird has a striking plumage pattern, look at how the feathers, individually and collectively, produce the effect.

## Flying high

Bird wings and tails are obviously designed for flight, but they're modified for other activities as well. Consider, for instance, the different wing characteristics of flying and diving birds. Long flight feathers and hollow bones can make wings as buoyant as corks, less than ideal for diving birds. To dive well, flightless penguin wings are reduced to mere flippers with no flight feathers at all. But to allow albatrosses to remain airborne for days at a time, their wings are extremely long—so buoyant they cannot dive under water. To allow loons to dive and fly both, their wings strike a critical medium, reducing the wing's

**Feather types**

The chart on the next page illustrates five very different types of feathers.

# TYPES OF FEATHERS

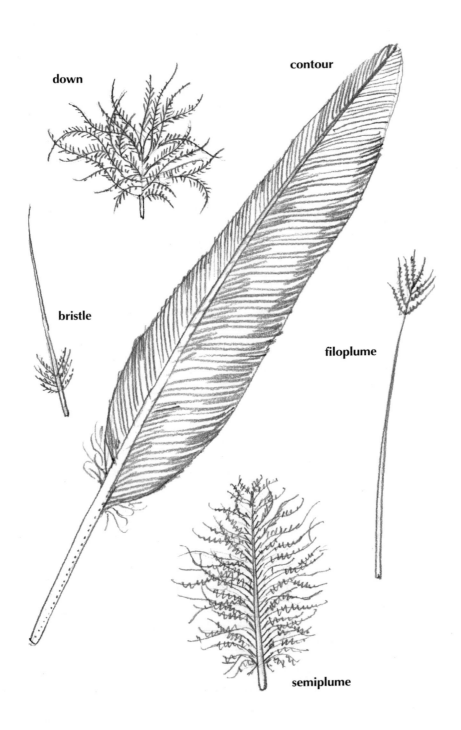

down

contour

bristle

filoplume

semiplume

© Pfeifer-Hamilton Publishers • 210 West Michigan • Duluth, MN 55810      (218) 727-0500

surface area. Loon wings are so small that a loon must run into a headwind as much as a quarter mile along the water's surface, beating its wings furiously, to get aloft. To stay airborne, it must keep flapping and maintain a high speed—Common Loons have been clocked at between 53 and 62 m.p.h. If a loon loses only one or two primary wing feathers, that wing's surface area may drop below the critical point, becoming too small to support flight. Loons replace flight feathers only once a year, during winter, spending their flightless period on the ocean.

The longer wings are, the more work it takes to flap them, but the more distance they cover with a single flap. Birds that migrate long distances usually have longer wings than closely-related nonmigrants.

Examine the feathers on a bird wing. The *primaries* are attached to the hand bones. (Birds technically have just about all the hand bones we do, but they're fused and don't look anything like ours.) A few little feathers are attached to the "thumb" part of the hand—these feathers are called the *alula*, and help birds stay aloft during slow, labored flight. The *secondaries* are attached to the *ulna*. (As in humans, the ulna is one of the two long bones between the elbow and wrist.) Hummingbirds and albatrosses both have ten primaries, but hummers have only six or seven secondaries while some albatrosses have over thirty. Because of their length and shape, primary feathers were usually the feather of choice for writing quills. The shiny, iridescent patch on duck wings, the *speculum*, is part of the secondaries. In hawks, owls, and ravens, the vanes of many primary feathers are noticeably narrow at the outer tip, so when the wings are fully opened, the primaries produce a fingered effect, called *wing slots*, for greater flight control.

Owl flight and body feathers are velvety soft to help muffle their sound in flight. Even more important for silent flight, the leading edge of an owl's first primary has short, stiff barbs spaced farther apart than other barbs. When the

**Shhh . . .**
Owl feathers are designed for silent flight.

wing swoops down, air is forced over the leading edge in many tiny flows rather than one large flow. Tiny flows make much less noise than the whoosh of air around a similar-sized wing of other species.

The bases of primaries and secondaries are covered by shorter feathers called *coverts*. If you tear out the coverts, you can see how and where the primaries and secondaries are anchored to bones. You can also see why coverts are necessary to keep the surface smooth and solid. Look at the overall curve of the wing and how the leading edge is thicker and stiffer than the trailing edge. This shape is what produces *lift*.

Tail feathers help a flying bird steer, brake, and rise on air currents. Ducks, having very short tails, can't turn corners as sharply as hawks. Fancy tail feathers, such as those of the Scissor-tailed Flycatcher, are used in nuptial or territorial displays as well as for precise maneuvers in catching airborne insects. Woodpeckers and swifts have spiny tail feathers, which they use to brace themselves against tree trunks. Some birds such as Eastern Kingbirds and Cedar Waxwings have a contrasting color at the tip of the tail. Many warblers have conspicuous tail spots. Finch tails usually have two sharply-pointed tips. Cuckoo tails have a rounded tip.

Tail feathers are attached to a broad bone at the end of the spinal column. This bone, called the *pygostyle*, is actually several vertebrae fused together. The bases of tail feathers are covered by tail coverts. The lower tail coverts blend into the *crissum*, which covers the bird's *vent* (the opening to the *cloaca*, where eggs and excreta are released), and the upper coverts blend into the *rump*. Some upper tail coverts, such as those of the Yellow-rumped Warbler, are brightly colored. The Palm Warbler's crissum is bright yellow, and the Gray Catbird's is rusty.

## Beaks

The words *beak* and *bill* are synonymous, but are sometimes used differently. From the sound of the words, beaks seem sharper than bills—we think of a cardinal's beak but a duck's bill. Beaks are composed of an upper and lower mandible.

Birds use beaks as tools to maintain their feathers, protect themselves, build nests, and most importantly, to obtain and ingest food.

Each group of birds has a distinctive bill, its shape related to the bird's feeding needs. The picture on the next page illustrates a variety of beaks. Humans design tools to do many of the same jobs as bird beaks perform. Like a strainer, duck bills drain water out of a mouthful of aquatic plants and animals. A grosbeak's bill works like a nutcracker, and a Brown Creeper's like tweezers. Woodpeckers have a chisel, oystercatchers a pry, hummingbirds a drinking straw, loons and herons a spear, mergansers a saw, and pelicans a pouch. It's easy to design a matching game with household tools and pictures of birds.

Mounted birds and museum specimens allow close inspection of a huge variety of bills. To study a very specialized beak, examine an American Woodcock—one of my hunting friends once cleaned out a whole woodcock skull for me, which I use a lot with kids. When woodcocks are alive, they eat earthworms which they pull from deep in the soil with their extremely long bill. Normal bird bills are rigid from base to tip, but a woodcock would face a serious problem if its bill were entirely rigid—if its mouth were shut when it reached two inches into the soil, it would have a hard time opening the beak to grab a worm against the force of compacted soil, but if it probed into the soil with its beak slightly open, it would end up with a mouthful of mud. Fortunately, woodcocks have a special adaptation—their beak is *prehensile*, allowing them to open just the tip to grab the worm while the rest of the mouth stays shut. When a woodcock dies, its beak stiffens, but you can still see little ridges where it once opened.

If you're working on a bird that hasn't dried out or been prepared for exhibit, open its beak and look into the mouth. If this is a species that catches flying insects on the wing, such as

**Birds don't chew.**
Beaks aren't designed for chewing—many birds swallow food in fairly large chunks, leaving it to their muscular stomach, or gizzard, to grind it up. An owl can swallow a whole chipmunk!

121

# BIRD BEAK SHAPES

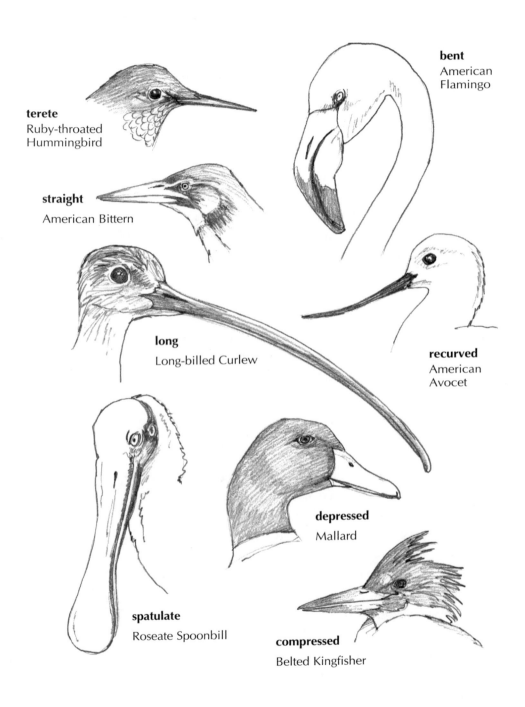

**terete**
Ruby-throated
Hummingbird

**bent**
American
Flamingo

**straight**
American Bittern

**long**
Long-billed Curlew

**recurved**
American
Avocet

**depressed**
Mallard

**spatulate**
Roseate Spoonbill

**compressed**
Belted Kingfisher

© Pfeifer-Hamilton Publishers  •  210 West Michigan  •  Duluth, MN 55810          (218) 727-0500

a nighthawk, swallow, or swift, the gape may be huge. Look at the roof of the mouth. Birds have a cleft palate where air passes to the trachea. This is open to the nostrils, too, so most birds can't create a vacuum to suck—to drink, they fill their beak with water and let it dribble down their throat. Doves and pigeons can close this palate to make it airtight, so they suck up their water.

Food goes down the bird's throat at the back of the mouth, often pushed by the tongue. All bird tongues are shaped to "fit the bill," but they often have unique and even fascinating features. Songbirds usually have an arrowhead-shaped tongue attached by a stalk to the back of the mouth. Hummingbird tongues look like gossamer thread, but under a microscope are quite complex—the tip is fringed (perhaps for lapping up nectar or entangling tiny insects), and the length of the tongue is rolled into two tubes, rather like a microscopic coffee stirrer. Nectar is either sucked through the tongue like a drinking straw or pulled up by capillary action. Some woodpecker tongues have a stiff tip that spears insects and pulls them out of deep tree crevices after the beak cuts into the wood, but sapsucker tongues are fringed to lap up sap. Many duck tongues are amazingly complex, with bizarre fringes and ridges for entangling aquatic plants and animals. Fish-eating birds often have little more than a tiny, useless flap for a tongue.

Many or all birds have the ability to taste, but unless you're working with slides of prepared histological samples of bird tongues, you won't detect taste buds.

At the top of the beak are the nostrils. In many birds, small bristle feathers cover and protect the nostrils. The nostrils vary in shape in different species. Ornithologists have long accepted that vultures and some oceanic birds have a well-developed sense of smell, and current research indicates that other birds also have a pretty good sense of smell. Cedar Waxwings detect odors better than Tree Swallows, probably because waxwings need to

The chart on the next page illustrates several kinds of bird feet. They're quite different but all clearly belong to birds.

recognize spoiled berries while swallows gulp down flying insects without any time to sniff first.

**Feet**

Most birds have four toes—three in front and one behind is the most common arrangement. The back toe is longer in birds that perch on branches. For example, herons, which nest in trees, have a long back toe whereas cranes, which sit only on the ground or in shallow water, have a tiny back toe. In some species, skin grows between the toes forming a web. In loons and ducks, webs run between the front toes *(palmate)*. In some shorebirds, the web is short *(semipalmate)*. In pelicans and cormorants, the web also runs between the outer front toe and the back toe *(totipalmate)*. Some swimming birds don't have webbed feet. Try to find a specimen of a grebe or a coot—each of their toes has funny looking lobes.

Woodpeckers and parrots (including cockatiels and budgies), climb up tree trunks, bracing themselves with both a stiff tail and two back toes, and have only two toes in front. Birds in animated Disney movies often have these *zygodactylous* feet, perhaps because Disney artists see more captive parrots than wild songbirds. Chimney Swifts cling to the insides of chimneys or hollow trees—their stiff tail braces them, and all four tiny toes face forward *(pamprodactyl)*. Mousebirds, from Africa, are also pamprodactyl—they can hang batlike from branches. But one of their toes is *opposable*, like our thumb, to support them when they perch normally.

Eagles, hawks, falcons, and owls have *talons*, muscular toes armed with lethal claws. They all have three toes in front and one in back, but one of the front toes of osprey and owls is opposable, and the four toes are all fairly close to the same length. A Bald Eagle clutches a fish with all six front toes on one side and the two hind toes on the other, while an Osprey clutches fish with the four normal front toes on one side and the hind toes and "thumb" toes on the other, an excellent balance that

# Bird Foot Shapes

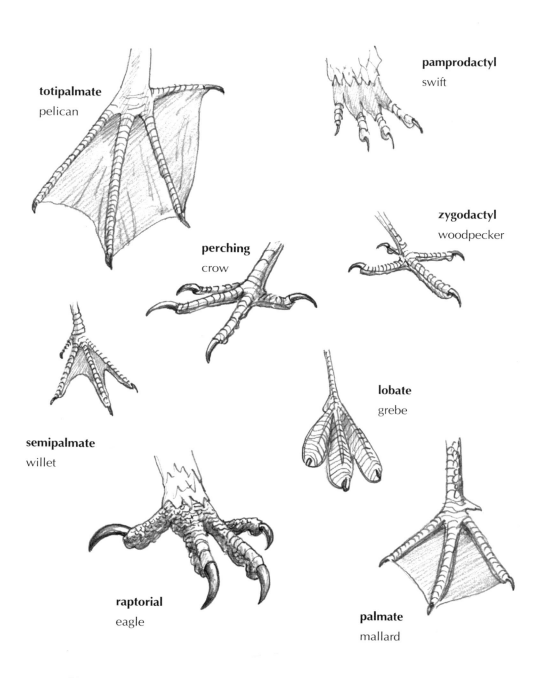

**totipalmate**
pelican

**pamprodactyl**
swift

**zygodactyl**
woodpecker

**perching**
crow

**lobate**
grebe

**semipalmate**
willet

**raptorial**
eagle

**palmate**
mallard

© Pfeifer-Hamilton Publishers  •  210 West Michigan  •  Duluth, MN 55810                    (218) 727-0500

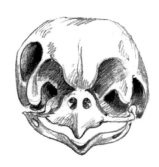

**Owl skull**

Examine the asymmetric ear openings.

holds even a desperately thrashing fish securely. Compared to the eagle's smoother toes, the bottom of Osprey toes is rough, covered with spiny scales called *spicules*. So Bald Eagles are more likely to drop their fish than Osprey are. In Alaska, an eagle once dropped a fish while flying above an airplane. The fish tore through the fuselage, and the pilot had to make an emergency landing. This is the only known case of a midair collision between a plane and a fish. The pilot, passengers, and eagle all survived—the only fatality was the fish.

In winter, the bottoms of grouse feet are covered with little ridges called *pectinations*. People once believed these held grouse above the snow like snowshoes, but most authorities now believe they serve as grippers, holding grouse securely on icy tree branches. The center toe of a nighthawk is also pectinated and serves as a handy comb for grooming.

### Other things to look at on a dead bird

Children are fascinated by bird ears. If you hold aside the cheek feathers, you'll see a hole in the bird's head with an interesting arrangement of bones. On some birds, especially owls, these ears are so enormous that through them you can see the back of the eye, which is a dark grayish blue. Owl ears are asymmetric, one higher and one further forward than the other. This helps owls to precisely locate prey in the dark because sounds reach one ear microseconds before the other. The feathers around an owl's ears grow in a lovely circular pattern, hiding the ears and focusing sound waves like a satellite dish.

Look at the bird's eyelids. In most species, the lower lid is larger than the upper, but not in the owl and nighthawk families. Forward-facing, blinking eyes contribute to an owl's humanlike aspect. In dead birds, sometimes you can find the inner eyelid, or *nictitating membrane*. (The pink tissue in the corner of the human eye near the nose is the remnant of this membrane.)

If you're dealing with a prepared specimen, the eye itself

will be gone—in a mount prepared by a taxidermist, it has been replaced with a plastic eye, and on a "study specimen" cotton shows through the eye hole. If you have a dead bird that was frozen, the fluids in the eye have probably crystallized, distorting its appearance.

Look beneath rump feathers for a large pimplelike bump—that's the *oil gland*. Birds rub this gland with their beak while preening and then coat their feathers with the oil.

Look at your bird's abdomen. In spring and summer, many female birds develop a *brood patch*—a bare area on the belly hidden by neighboring contour feathers. If the feathers were left in place, they'd hold body heat away from eggs or nestlings, so during the breeding season females of some species tear them out; in other species hormone levels cause the feathers to fall out on their own. Banders can often determine whether birds are breeding females by blowing on their tummies to see if there's a brood patch. In the Disney movie *Snow White*, the wicked witch's pet crow is a breeding female—you can see the brood patch for a split second when the witch adds a gust of wind to her evil brew.

The sternum of all North American birds is a keel bone, shaped like the front of a canoe. The *pectoral*, or breast, muscles flesh out the keel, making the breast feel full and round in healthy birds. When birds are starving, they absorb the pectorals, and eventually the keel bone juts out sharply. Banders and bird rehabilitators feel the breast muscle to determine a bird's general condition.

## Digging deeper

When I work on a dissection with kids, we often spend an hour or so studying the dead bird before we actually start cutting. But eventually we exhaust the possibilities and want to probe deeper. Whether you're doing this with your own child or demonstrating the dissection for a large class, or whether

**Grounded birds**

Flightless running birds such as ostriches, kiwis, and emus are called *ratites*—their sternum is not shaped like a keel. Although they can fly, penguins have a keel to support the pectoral muscles they need for swimming with their flippers.

children are working on their own or in pairs, someone has to make the first cut.

The skin of birds is much thinner and more fragile than mammal skin—especially in owls and the nighthawk family. Remove some of the breast and belly feathers and make a clean cut through the thin layer of breast skin, pulling it away to expose the pectoral muscles. Look at how these muscles attach to the wing bones to power flight. Move the wings back and forth to see how the muscles work.

There are two broad types of muscle fibers, white and red. "White meat" is made up of many more white than red fibers, and "dark meat" of more red than white. Birds needing sustained muscle power for long-distance flight need a constant blood and oxygen supply and plenty of mitochondria in their muscle cells, so their flight muscles consist mostly of red fibers. Songbirds, ducks, and geese all have dark pectoral muscles—in sparrows and hummingbirds, every single muscle fiber is red. Birds that fly more rarely and don't travel long distances but do need a quick escape when a predator appears may conserve energy with breast muscles composed of many more white muscle fibers than red. These don't require such rich blood and oxygen supplies but can produce an enormous burst of speed for short periods—handy for tasty birds with many enemies. Chickens, turkeys, and grouse have mostly white pectoral muscle fibers.

The sternum and breast muscles are thick enough to make it difficult to hear a living bird's heart even with a stethoscope against the chest. Veterinarians and rehabilitators usually listen to the heart from the back. When you tell kids this, they often ask to take a listen before they think it through. Dead birds are usually pretty quiet.

After you examine the pectoral muscles, remove and weigh them. A hummingbird's pectoral muscles usually comprise an amazing 25 to 30 percent of the bird's total weight.

Before opening the body cavity, you may want to compare

the leg muscles with the pectorals. Open the skin from the belly through the length of one leg. Bird "knees" really do face forward as ours do, but they are too close to the body to be seen easily when the bird is alive. What we call the "leg" on a running or hopping robin is really comparable to our foot, and what we call its "foot" is really its toes. What looks like a backward knee is really its ankle. Birds that use their legs often—for swimming or walking—have many red fibers in their leg muscles.

When relaxed, bird toes close tightly, keeping birds from falling off branches while asleep. *Flexor tendons* in the bird's legs run down to the toes, locking them shut. Cut off a leg at the top of the lowest segment. Find the cut ends of the flexor tendons and pull them to see how they work the toes. Tendons don't need much blood supply at all compared to muscles. Songbirds have so little blood in their feet and so little water in the hard tissues of their feet and toes that they never need pack boots to avoid frostbite. Doves and pigeons have fleshier feet that are susceptible to frostbite.

## The inside scoop

The *sternum*, or breastbone, in flying birds is a solid keel bone, a relatively huge structure designed to support the flight muscles. Examine the shape of it inside the bird. The wings are supported by a tripod of bones. The heaviest, the *coracoids*, rest on the sternum. Suspended from, and sometimes attached to, the coracoids is the *furcula* (wishbone), comparable to our collarbone. The *scapula* is a thin, bladelike bone embedded in muscles along the side of the spinal column. Work the wings again to see how the bones move. Carefully cut the keel where it narrows at the sides, and pull it out.

Now you're seeing organs! Notice how well everything fits together. The dark red organ, which is the biggest organ in many birds, is the *liver*. The *glandular stomach* is grayer and more squishy, unless the bird died while digesting a really big meal. Some species have a prominent gizzard, or *muscular stomach*,

**Old-fashioned toys**

Long ago, when parents butchered a chicken or turkey, they gave their children bird feet to play with: the kids tugged on the flexor tendons to open and close the feet.

**Creating scientists**

Let kids guess how things work, then show them whether they're right. Even better, help them figure out how to test their guess rather than simply telling them.

while in others the gizzard may be hard to distinguish from the glandular stomach. The gizzard is tucked between the glandular stomach and the *intestines*, which are relatively short in birds. The heart should be tucked in there, too. But where are the lungs? Ask kids to make guesses—let this be a mystery for a bit. Don't cut any organs out just yet.

First, look at the neck. Kids will be amazed at how long and skinny it is. Three structures run down the neck: the *spinal column*, which is vertebrae bones covered with muscles through which the white spinal cord runs; the *esophagus*, which is smooth and muscular (and can often stretch amazingly to let large chunks of food pass through); and the *trachea*, a whitish, ringed tube which branches into the bronchial tubes to send air into the lungs. Turn the bird's head to see how the neck snakes around more than twists. See if you can locate the *carotid arteries*, which supply blood to the brain. They run on each side of the spinal column, fitting in narrow grooves.

## Respiration

Now back to our mysterious lungs: Bird and mammal lungs are strikingly different. When you dissect a mammal, the lungs are among the most conspicuous organs in the chest cavity. When mammals inhale, air goes into tiny dead-end sacs called *alveoli* deep inside the lungs, so mammal lungs inflate and deflate with each breath. A lot of air remains in these alveoli after exhalation, so lung tissue is very light and airy compared with other internal organs.

Birds need their heaviest, not lightest, organs near their center of gravity. They also need a more efficient respiratory system than mammals do to allow them to fly and remain active at high altitudes where oxygen levels are low. When you open the chest cavity of a bird, you can't see the lungs—they're small and flat, next to or even fused against the back ribs. Avian lungs don't expand and contract with breathing. Rather, inhaled air passes right through them into enormous, balloonlike *air sacs* that fill spaces throughout the body, allowing each inhalation to take in a huge quantity of air. Avian lungs take up oxygen quickly and efficiently, but so much air passes through that there's plenty of oxygen left to be absorbed on exhalation, too.

But don't root around searching for the lungs until later, or you'll miss the best part of the whole dissection—checking out the air sacs. Stick a straw through your dead bird's mouth into its trachea; blow gently into it, and the air sacs will inflate. This is one of the most impressive sights in a bird dissection, and the kids (and you if you've never seen this before) will be amazed. The air sacs in living birds always have at least some volume of air in them, so dead birds really are smaller than living ones.

Air sacs serve many purposes besides just holding and moistening respired air. They help release excess body heat. Loons and grebes can slowly deflate their air sacs, making their bodies more and more dense so they can slowly sink into the water. In species such as pelicans, that plunge into deep water from high in the air, a neck air sac feeds smaller ones beneath the neck and breast skin to cushion against the force of impact so they won't "belly-flop." Air sacs sometimes put pressure on the voice box to aid in sound production, and in male grouse and prairie chickens, special air sacs outside the body are uniquely adapted for breeding displays.

Examine the trachea. As in mammals, the rings prevent the airway from collapsing and sticking shut like a deflated balloon. The larynx of a bird is a simple thickening of the trachea that may not even be visible. Birds produce their songs through a more complicated "song box" right where the trachea splits into the bronchial tubes. Complex muscles allow this *syrinx* to produce complex songs—thrushes can produce two different sounds simultaneously, providing their own harmony. These muscles are small and difficult to study with the

**Take a deep breath**

Air sacs of preserved specimens from biological supply houses become tough and seldom inflate properly. Fresh or frozen specimens show this avian miracle much more clearly.

**The milk of kindness**

Mammals are the only animals that produce milk in mammary glands, but a few kinds of birds, including doves, pigeons, penguins, and flamingos, feed their young a fluid produced in the esophagus that is similar to milk. This "pigeon's milk," like real milk, is rich in fat and proteins and is produced in response to prolactin, the same hormone that stimulates milk production in humans and other mammals.

naked eye, but kids can use their imaginations and look at diagrams in books.

## Digestion

Now probe from the mouth into the esophagus, looking at the distensible food tube. On the outside, use the probe and forceps to trace the path that food follows from the esophagus to the stomach and intestines. You'll probably need to remove the liver, that big, dense, red organ with noticeable lobes. Weigh it.

Bird digestive systems vary widely, depending on diet. The esophagus often has one or two offshoot pouches called *crops*. In doves, the crop produces special fat cells that slough off to form the "pigeon's milk" they feed their nestlings. Seed-eating birds may have a well-developed crop or many smaller esophageal pouches for storing food—they stuff themselves before bed on frigid nights and digest all night long, stoking their metabolic furnace to keep warm.

Food passes from the esophagus and crop to the *glandular stomach*, where hydrochloric acid and an enzyme called pepsin begin breaking down food. Secretions in a hawk's glandular stomach are acidic enough to dissolve bones. From the glandular stomach, food passes to the *muscular stomach*, or *gizzard*, where food is ground up mechanically with the aid of grit or stones. In owls, the bones and fur or feathers of their prey collect in the gizzard and get compacted, to be spit out as a pellet. The stomachs of some birds are surprisingly enormous.

From the stomach, food passes to the intestines, where bile from the liver and secretions from the pancreas continue the digestion process. The pancreas is a long pink organ that fits elegantly into a fold of the small intestine. Grouse, which eat aspen buds and branch tips in winter, need extra long intestines to digest the woody tissue. Birds that eat fruits or soft-bodied insects have fairly short intestines. At the juncture between the small and large intestine (where our appendix is), some birds have two dead-end offshoots called *caeca*. In grouse, the caeca harbor bacteria that break down cellulose—the caeca grow very large in winter when woody tissue makes up much of the diet. Nighthawks and whip-poor-wills have caeca, too, possibly to digest the hard exoskeletons of beetles and other insects. The large intestine, or rectum, is short and empties into the *cloaca*, a chamber designed to hold food wastes for a very short time, extracting water and then expelling the waste. The cloaca is also the chamber where: 1) urine collects to be excreted, 2) sperm leaves a male and enters a female during mating, and 3) eggs come out of a laying hen—sort of an all-purpose room. The door out of the cloaca is called the *vent*.

## Circulation

After you've removed some of the digestive organs, the heart should be plainly visible. A bird's heart is similar to a mammal's, with four chambers, but the right aortic arch is present rather than the left. In comparisons between birds and similar-size mammals, the avian heart is about 40 percent larger. The rate of a resting hummingbird's heartbeat is about 615 beats per minute—when active, that probably doubles. A pigeon's heart rate is about 220 beats per minute, a House Wren's 700.

## Elimination

Birds have two kidneys (way in back, below or near the lower ribs), usually divided into three major lobes. Impurities in the blood are filtered by the kidneys and then pass through the ureters into the cloaca to mix with intestinal waste. A urinary bladder would be excess baggage in a creature that needs to fly.

Kids (and grown-ups) are often intrigued with the color of bird droppings. Droppings aren't all white—the whitewash (the bird's urine) encircles a dark center (the intestinal waste). Why is the urine white? The waste from biological processes and dead cells carried by blood to the kidneys is composed of many chemicals, some made with nitrogen. In mammal kidneys, these nitrogenous wastes are converted to

**Rated R**

The sex organs of most wild birds shrink after the breeding season, so are hard to find. But many pigeons remain in breeding readiness throughout the year, so the sex of a preserved pigeon from a biological supply house will be easy to determine after the digestive organs are removed (as long as the bird was a fully-developed adult). If the specimen is male, its two testes will look like pale beans. The single ovary of a female, on the left side, looks like a tiny cluster of grapes.

*urea*, a somewhat toxic chemical that must be diluted with lots of water. Even unborn babies produce urea which they release into the amniotic fluid. The mother's kidneys filter this waste with her own. If unhatched chicks produced urea, the egg would have no way of diluting it or getting rid of it. So avian kidneys convert nitrogenous wastes to *uric acid* instead. Uric acid is toxic too, but when concentrated precipitates into a chalky white solid that won't hurt the developing chick. Because birds and reptiles develop in eggs, their kidneys produce uric acid rather than urea. Uric acid needs to be diluted with less water than urea, and so uric acid has the added benefit of conserving water after hatching as well as before.

## Reproduction

Although some grown-ups equate sex education with the birds and the bees, the insides of most bird bodies won't teach kids much of anything about reproduction. Few male birds have a penis at all—at most, some have a "cloacal protuberance." During most of the year, the internal sex organs are diminished in size and are often too small for even professional ornithologists to locate. If you can't find the sex organs or can't figure out whether your bird is a male or a female, don't panic.

Male birds have two testes which are usually in the body cavity at the anterior end of each kidney. Sperm passes from the testes through the vas deferens to the cloaca. Females usually have only the left ovary and oviduct—probably both to reduce weight and to prevent two eggs from cracking into each other inside. Falcons and some hawks may have an undeveloped right ovary, but only the left oviduct. Sperm leaves the male's cloaca and enters the female's in the act of copulation, which ornithologists romantically call the "cloacal kiss." Eggs pass through the stretchable oviduct to the cloaca, and then out they go through the vent.

## Nervous system

A bird's brain is a bit smaller and smoother than the brain of a similar-size mammal, perhaps because birds are less intelligent than mammals but more likely because they've somehow managed to make their brains more efficient to accommodate the complex needs of flight—a Sharp-shinned Hawk's brain not only needs to process sights to detect prey in the first place, it must also coordinate its movements to avoid tree branches while in full pursuit of its prey, a bird with an even smaller brain that usually manages to evade the sharpie successfully by keeping track of where it is even as it darts and weaves through forest branches. Chickadee brains are known to grow new neurons to replace old ones every fall, right when chickadees need to memorize new food storage places. Storing memories of every crevice in a birch tree years after the tree was chopped down would waste valuable brain space. We humans may think we're smarter, but my personal brain space is brimming with worthless knowledge—I can recite a Chicago phone number, Hudson 3-2700, from a radio commercial back in the 1950s, even though I don't have a clue whose number it was. I also remember an entire jingle beginning, "At three in the morning when you're in bed, the Holsum bakers are baking bread." Birds may have little brains, but they sure don't waste valuable neuron space with the theme song to "The Beverly Hillbillies" decades after the show was canceled.

Before you even try to look at the brain, tease the skin off the head to look at the skull. Although bird brains are fascinating, you probably won't be able to figure out much about them as you dissect the head. The simplest way to see the brain on most birds is to peek through the translucent skull. The brain will be a tiny organ that fits between the huge eyes and the ears. Brains fall apart easily, and just getting through the skull without rupturing them is a real trick. Eyeballs are also difficult to work on, but you shouldn't have any trouble seeing how enormous the eye is in the skull—far

### Bird brains

Little bird brains come equipped with map, compass, calendar, feeding and maintenance instructions, and other important knowledge.

**Owl-eye activity**

To help kids imagine what it would be like to see with owl eyes, which are fixed in their sockets, have the kids hold two toilet paper tubes up to their eyes and follow a small bright object as you carry it from place to place. They'll move their head and neck in the same way that owls do to keep the object in view.

bigger than it appears from the outside. Notice how little the eye can move within the socket. Owl eyes are tubular and can't move at all. Also note how the eyes are positioned. Woodcock and nighthawk eyes can see above and behind as well as ahead. Brown Creeper eyes are set forward for close range binocular vision as they creep up tree trunks.

## The incredible, edible egg

Eggs we buy in supermarkets are usually unfertilized, so examining (or eating!) store-bought eggs doesn't hurt an embryo. When you hold a light up to a developing fertilized egg, you may see shadows showing the chick's development—this process is called *candling*. If you take a field trip to a poultry farm, someone may candle eggs to show the children several stages of development. Some people who run bluebird trails also candle eggs.

Whether you're looking at an egg from a chicken, an ostrich, or a hummingbird, the yolk is a single cell, the *ovum*. The ovum begins as a tiny germinal cell within a follicle of the ovary. As hormones prepare the follicle for ovulation, the yolk accumulates. After ovulation, the yolk-filled ovum passes down the oviduct. If sperm are present in the oviduct, one may fertilize it.

Whether or not the ovum gets fertilized, the walls of the oviduct secrete *albumen* (the egg white) around it, eventually making a dense coating. Further down the oviduct, the albumen is coated with a blend of calcium and other chemicals which will form the *shell*. When the egg reaches the cloaca it's expelled, presumably when the bird is sitting on a nest. Normally, a bird doesn't start developing eggs until her courting and nest-building activities signal her hormones to kick in, but sometimes duck eggs are ready before the nest is. Then the female quickly finds someone else's nest to lay her eggs in. The ostrich lays them on the ground, and Ogden Nash pointed out that "It has such long and lofty legs, I'm glad it sits to lay its eggs."

The egg is nature's starkest efficiency apartment. The yolk serves as the apartment's pantry, holding a rich mixture of fats, proteins, and carbohydrates to nourish the embryo. The egg white, or albumen, serves as an all-encompassing waterbed for the ultimate couch potato. It cushions the embryo, protects it from drying out, and provides structural support to keep the yolk from flattening. The albumen is comprised of about 88 percent water and 10 percent amino acids, along with traces of various minerals. The albumen transfers water and nutrients to the yolk as the chick develops. Egg proteins are easily denatured when exposed to heat or air, which is why eggs cook as they do.

The shell protects the egg, keeps it from drying out, and provides ventilation through hundreds of tiny pores where oxygen and carbon dioxide diffuse in and out. If the shell serves as the apartment walls, the pores are the windows.

As the chick develops, its wastes collect in the egg's bathroom—an air bubble chamber called the *allantois*, which grows as the yolk shrinks. The allantois is surrounded by a network of blood vessels. As the chick grows, these thin-walled vessels press against the shell, absorbing oxygen through the pores, and allowing the chick to solve its waste disposal and breathing problems in one simple system. Uric acid produced by the growing chick forms a chalky deposit you might be able to find against the broken shell of a hatched egg.

## Owl pellets

Owls swallow their prey whole or in large chunks. The glandular stomach's secretions are acidic enough to break down muscle, skin, organ, and cartilaginous tissue, but not as acidic as a hawk's stomach secretions—not acidic enough to break down bones, feathers, or fur. These materials can't pass from the gizzard into the intestines; periodically the owl regurgitates them in a neat little package called a *pellet*.

If you show children an owl pellet, one kid or another will invariably comment that it looks like poop, but owl pellets are

**Owl pellets**

You can find complete bird and rodent skeletons in regurgitated owl pellets.

surprisingly clean and odorless. Since they haven't passed through the intestines, they have absolutely none of the bacteria or odors associated with feces. The fur in a pellet has been felted, but falls apart easily to reveal tiny bones. Kits with pellets along with drawings of the various types of bones and skulls that might be found in them are available from biological supply houses. (See Chapter 2.)

Kids love picking pellets apart, identifying the bones, and assembling tiny skeletons. The best tools to use are a couple of toothpicks—kids usually don't have a delicate enough touch to use forceps. Attach the skeletons to index cards with white glue. School teachers should ask kids to each bring in a margarine container ahead of time: most kids will want to bring their bones home, and if they're put in a plastic bag, they'll get crushed in their backpacks. Wrap them with a paper towel or tissue paper before placing them in the container.

Owl pellets usually contain two or three entire skeletons, but invariably at least one child will find an extra skull. How did that come about? The kids will make guesses: Did the owl eat a two-headed mouse? Was part of the mouse in another pellet regurgitated at an earlier or later time? Did the rest of the mouse actually get digested? These are all great hypotheses. You won't be able to experiment in class to prove it, but the explanation for the extra skull is that after the owl has eaten two or three mice in a night, it gets full, but not too full to grab another mouse if the opportunity arises. Now it isn't hungry enough to eat the whole thing, so it just gobbles down its favorite part—the head—for dessert. Kids love this.

## Kitchen biology

Look at an ordinary egg through a magnifying glass or backward binoculars to see how rough the shell is. Can you see pores? When you carefully crack it open, notice how the yolk, albumen, and shell are all discrete entities separated by thin membranes. You may be able to see tiny blood vessels on part of the yolk—that's where the germinal spot is.

An air bubble is the allantois. Cooking an egg denatures the protein molecules, hardening and thickening them and turning them opaque white. Beating an egg white does the same thing, but mixing it with so much air that it becomes foamy.

After one dissection unit in science class, some of my sixth-grade boys bought a dead chicken from a poultry farm, head and feet still intact. At home, they boiled off the meat, cleaned the bones, and tried to reconnect the skeleton with wires, apparently having at least one set of parents with a sense of humor. This project was the kids' own idea, so they were excited and motivated, even borrowing some of my college ornithology textbooks to see how the bones were supposed to go back together. The end product didn't look quite as perfect as they envisioned, but they learned a lot about anatomy and created a memorable sculpture.

Next time you prepare a broiler chicken or a turkey, see how many body parts are identifiable. Both lower legs and feet are cut off before marketing, as is the head. The muscle-covered vertebrae of the neck are usually packed in the body cavity, but the esophagus and trachea are missing. The lungs are usually gone from the back, and the fragile air sacs will certainly be missing. You can often see traces of the kidneys just below the ribs. The heart, liver, and muscular stomach (gizzard) are usually packed inside in a little bag, but the glandular stomach and intestines are not. You can see the pimplelike papillae where feathers sprouted on the skin. Can you identify feather tracts or apteria?

Compare the breast meat, dominated by white muscle fibers, with the dark meat, dominated by red fibers. Usually you're not supposed to taste biology projects, but in this case, you might make an exception. After you've cleaned off the meat, look at the breast bone's noticeable keel. Can you find the furcula? Make a wish!

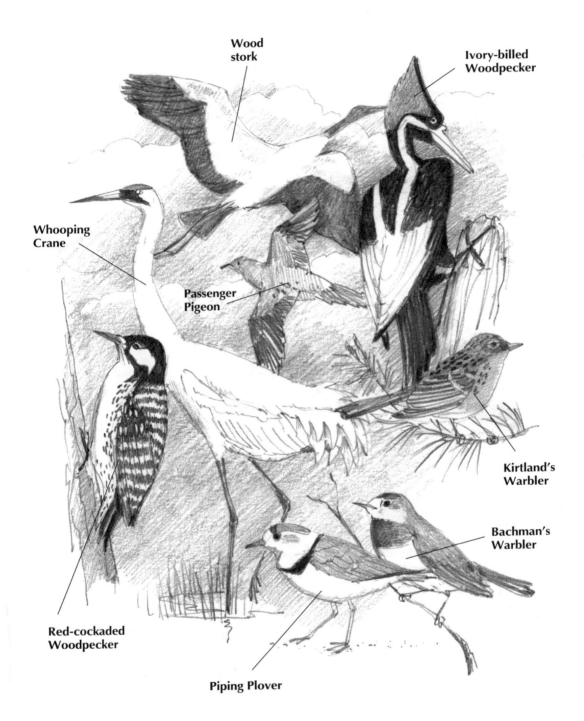

Wood stork

Ivory-billed Woodpecker

Whooping Crane

Passenger Pigeon

Kirtland's Warbler

Bachman's Warbler

Red-cockaded Woodpecker

Piping Plover

# 8

# Helping CHILDREN SAVE BIRDS

**H**ope is the thing with feathers that perches in the soul. Emily Dickenson understood how deeply our trust in the future is intertwined with the elemental beauty of birds. Is there any greater symbol of hope, of life itself, than that ultimate food for the soul—a bird's egg? Nature's most elegant package opens to reveal nature's most exquisite gift, feathered like an angel, capable of plunging deep into the ocean, fluttering delicately about the land, and soaring ever skyward, bridging water, earth, and air like no other creature on the planet. Terry Tempest Williams wrote in *Refuge*, "How can hope be denied when there is always the possibility of an American flamingo or a roseate spoonbill floating down from the sky like pink rose petals?"

Outside of zoos and aviaries, the only flamingos normally found in the United States are the plastic lawn variety, which are flourishing. But Roseate Spoonbills were almost wiped out in the first half of this century—by 1939, only thirty individuals remained in the entire state of Florida. It was faith and hope, along with the will and enforcement power of the United States government, that brought them back. By the late 1970s, 500–600 nesting pairs graced Florida wetlands once again. Texas and Louisiana populations stayed reasonably healthy, too.

But the Florida Everglades, that endless ocean of grass that

## Vanishing birds

Over the past decades, many birders and ornithologists have watched favorite common birds—nighthawks, martins, swallows, and others that used to be abundant—vanish or dwindle from their neighborhoods. What have we done to our children's legacy?

these pink grace notes depend upon, is endless no more. It has been reduced to tattered patches by irrigation and development, native sawgrass edged out and the habitat compromised by encroaching cattails. Since the 1970s, Orlando and Miami have swelled with growth, development, and an outpouring of sewage and agricultural runoff that leaks unabated into our national treasure. In the 1930s, Wood Storks numbered 4,000 breeding pairs in the Everglades; by 1993, only 25 pairs remained to breed in the park. The federal government's authority to regulate and enforce environmental protection is dwindling. Faith and hope aren't enough to protect the Everglades.

Many of our most precious birds are declining dangerously. In the two decades since I became a birder in 1975, the last pairs of Piping Plovers to breed on Lake Superior in Minnesota and Wisconsin have vanished. Grassland birds such as Greater and Lesser Prairie-Chickens, Northern Harriers, and Short-eared Owls seem to be in a tailspin over much or even most of their ranges. Every California Condor has died or been taken into captivity, the last Dusky Seaside Sparrows were lost in a hurricane, Bachman's Warbler has been all but declared extinct, and the Ivory-billed Woodpecker has officially disappeared forever.

Not all birds are in trouble, of course, and healthy populations include more than just crows, gulls, starlings, and pigeons. Wood Ducks, brought to the verge of extinction by market hunters and habitat destruction, bounced back thanks to nest box programs and federal hunting restrictions and now thrive as one of our most beautiful and beloved game birds. Bluebirds have increased wonderfully in many areas thanks to bluebird nest box projects. Since 1992 when the federal government, under the Nixon Administration, banned D.D.T., Osprey and Bald Eagles have recovered well. Although breeding Peregrine Falcons were extirpated from all of eastern North America by the late 1970s, peregrine reintroduction projects reintroduced many new pairs, which are nesting on cliffs and city buildings once again. Kirtland's Warbler numbers are double what they were in the 1970s.

But these rare success stories underscore the unsettling truth that other birds really are declining dangerously. Dr. Sidney Gauthreaux of Clemson University, analyzing military and weather radar data, discovered that between the 1960s and the 1980s the number of birds migrating along the Gulf of Mexico declined an incredible 50 percent. As the human population grows inexorably, the twenty-first century will undoubtedly see even more extinctions than the twentieth. We can close our eyes and pretend they're just birds with no significance to us, their deaths holding no implications for our own future. We can grab for all the gusto we can get, rushing out to see as many endangered species as possible before they disappear, so we can boast to our children that we saw a California Condor even if they cannot. We can wring our hands in despair, cursing the darkness. Or we can roll up our sleeves and do something about it, lighting at least one tiny candle of hope.

Events on the scale of human population growth and tropical deforestation are too big for any individual to control or perhaps even influence, but parents and teachers are empowered to change the world in two ways. First, it is we adults who open children's eyes to many things, who direct their gazes into tiny corners of knowledge that the children might not otherwise have noticed. Most people first heard about the Spotted Owl in the context of lost jobs for humans, and many people naturally choose jobs in this tragically polarizing issue—it would be inhuman by definition to value birds, or anything else, above human life. But if parents and teachers had known and explained to children a generation ago about the intricate food web of the Pacific Coast ancient forest, things might have gone differently, and much mean-spiritedness might have been avoided.

A tiny arboreal mouse of the Pacific rain forest eats fungus growing on the trunks of ancient trees. The Spotted Owl hunts

**Let's get to work**

At a critical juncture in our nation's history, John Adams said, "We cannot ensure success, but we can deserve it."

143

## Reduce, reuse, and recycle

Conserving paper and other wood products saves birds. Trees are renewable resources, but old forests that many birds need take much longer to regenerate than young forests clear-cut for paper and fiber. Foresters manage aspen trees on rotation cycles of forty years or less. After that, heart rot sets in, reducing the trees' commercial value. But still-healthy trees with rotten heartwood are perfect for flickers and Pileated Woodpeckers, who hack the outer wood as deep as their beaks can reach and then scoop out the soft, rotted inner wood for nest chambers. They use each nest hole for a year and then leave it for Wood Ducks, mergansers, small owls, and kestrels to nest in as long as the tree remains standing.

this mouse very effectively, but when fungus-laden ancient trees are chopped down and the mice that live in them disappear, Barred Owls edge out Spotted Owls.

A great many of the ancient trees that are chopped down in the Pacific forests aren't cut into lumber here in the United States, where they might provide jobs for our people. Rather, they're shipped to Japan as raw timber. Japan doesn't need so much wood right now, but they figure at the rate we're cutting our ancient forests down, the trees will be gone in decades, so the Japanese store our dead trees under the ocean to be used in the future, after the ancient forest has disappeared. Trees will certainly grow back, but it may take hundreds of years for them to get old enough to grow the fungus that supports the mouse that feeds the Spotted Owl. My children will be gone by then—I want them to enjoy ancient forests during their lives.

Ancient forests provide homes for creatures and plants besides owls, mice, and fungus. The yew plant growing in western forests was dismissed as a woody weed until medical researchers discovered that this plant we'd been squandering produces a chemical, *taxol*, that may cure a lethal human disease, ovarian cancer. It turns out that protecting nature helps people as well as owls. What other useful plants and animals might be lurking, undiscovered, in the ancient forest or in other habitats?

If children of earlier generations had grown up appreciating the fragility of relationships in the northern Pacific rain forest food web, perhaps they would have been motivated as adults to search harder for solutions that could protect owls and jobs both. The more understanding we bring to any problem, the wiser our solutions will be. When we teach children the names of birds, they begin to recognize and understand some of the rich variety of the natural world, which will ultimately help them appreciate the truth and value of Aldo Leopold's maxim, "To keep every cog and wheel is the first precaution of intelligent tinkering."

The second way that parents and teachers affect the world is by showing children how to face problems with hope and faith in the future. Even if others despair about declining bird populations and other environmental issues, parents, grandparents, and school teachers must not. People who love children are obligated to work to save the things that our children love and need. If we cannot prove by our actions that we value our children and strive to bequeath to them a beautiful world, who will? If we tell them the situation is hopeless and we can't make a difference anyway, they will feel betrayed by us, lost in despair and powerlessness.

As children grow in understanding about the many things that destroy birds in our modern world, they will need concrete ways that they can address at least some of those problems. We can't give them that unless we ourselves get a handle on the issues.

## Where have all the birds gone?

Countless things in modern America kill birds outright. Television and radio towers and lighted skyscrapers lure millions of migrating songbirds to their deaths. As many as 20,000 migrating birds were killed at one TV tower in Eau Claire, Wisconsin, on a single foggy September night in 1957. Picture windows kill at least 100 million birds in the U.S. annually, and highways and wind turbines kill millions more. Wires are apparently invisible to "eagle eyes." A U.S. Fish and Wildlife Service technical report concluded that 68 percent of waterfowl flying in the vicinity of power lines in the Great Plains don't see the lines. During my three-day visit to the Platte River in Nebraska in March 1996, researchers picked up seventeen dead cranes under one set of power lines stretched across the Platte River at the Annette Rowe Sanctuary—and who knows how many other fatally injured cranes limped away to die? Who knows how many dead and crippled ones were carried off by Bald Eagles and coyotes or washed away in the

**Offer hope to children**
Telling children success stories—about the comebacks of Eastern Bluebirds, Bald Eagles, and Wood Ducks, for example— gives them hope that birds currently in trouble may also stage comebacks.

**Simple solution**
Birds flying through unfamiliar territory either don't see or can't accurately gauge their distance from power lines and guy wires. It's often a simple matter to add balls or small "visibility coils" that will help this problem enormously. When the Annette Rowe Sanctuary and a local power company marked a power line with inexpensive visibility coils, mortality at that wire dropped to less than 25 percent of that at unmarked lines.

**Conserve water**

Every drop of clean water that comes from a faucet, toilet, hose, or irrigation line is taken from the natural world. Conserving clean water ensures future supplies for birds and humans both.

**Woodcutting for birds**

Avoid felling trees or pruning large limbs during nesting season. In the Upper Midwest, for example, prune before mid-May or wait until August.

river? What inhospitable treatment of this bird that provides Nebraska with millions of tourism dollars every year!

Dr. Stanley Temple, a prominent ecologist, estimated that house cats kill 38 million songbirds and 140,000 game birds every year—in Wisconsin alone! Introduced starlings and House Sparrows kill bluebirds, swallows, and woodpeckers that compete for the same nest holes. And many pesticides, including ones people still commonly use on lawns and golf courses— chemicals registered by the E.P.A.—are lethal to birds. Registered pesticides are considered innocent until proven guilty, and accounts of backyard birds killed by lawn sprays are usually dismissed as mere anecdotal evidence.

Even more insidious are the countless things that kill birds indirectly. Pesticides destroy not just birds, but also bird food. Once worms vanish from an area, what are robins to eat? What are they to feed their young? Filling and draining wetlands takes an enormous toll. Every discount department store built on a wetland has probably edged out at least one pair of Northern Harriers, along with rails, herons, and other marsh species. Every temporary pond that farmers drain to increase arable acreage takes a home from ducks.

Ironically, one of the greatest threats to many songbirds is another songbird. The Brown-headed Cowbird once roamed the Great Plains, following wandering bison from place to place. Cowbirds relied on the heavy-hoofed bison to cut through the dense prairie sod, exposing insects and seeds for the cowbirds to eat. During the nesting season, this dependence on buffalo would have been a problem if cowbirds nested as other birds do—when the bison moved on, how could a mother cowbird feed her nestlings, or herself for that matter?

But cowbirds don't nest as other birds do—they are *brood parasites*. Female cowbirds devote their maternal time and energy to searching for the nests of other smaller species. When one of these little birds leaves its nest in the morning, the cowbird sneaks in, tosses out one of the little bird's eggs, and deposits one of her own. The little bird incubates the cowbird egg with her own.

When hatched, the baby cowbird is bigger than the others. It doesn't toss other eggs or babies from the nest the way European cuckoos do, nor does it hurt its adopted brothers and sisters. But its insistent begging and huge mouth make it a more noticeable target for parent birds to feed, so it gets the lion's share of the food. One or two natural babies in the nest are also likely to survive, especially in years when food is abundant, but raising a cowbird significantly reduces the number of young raised to adulthood.

In the days of the great bison herds, cowbirds didn't affect bird populations. The bison wandered widely, and cowbirds were unlikely to parasitize the same birds more than once in a lifetime except in streamside areas where the bison spent a lot of time getting water. One of the birds that lives along streams, the Yellow Warbler, adapted to cowbirds by developing the ability to recognize cowbird eggs. A warbler's beak is too tiny to pick up and toss out a cowbird egg, but if these warblers do discover an intruder egg, they sometimes rebuild their nest on the spot—literally—by covering the old nest, eggs and all, with a new floor and laying more eggs. If a cowbird tries again, the warblers may build another floor and yet another—sometimes ending up with a nest five "stories" high. This is rather like throwing the baby out with the bathwater because the Yellow Warbler's own eggs are covered up as well, but overall the process does maximize baby warbler production.

When the bison were extirpated, cowbirds didn't disappear with them for two reasons. First, humans introduced a substitute—domestic cattle—which the cowbirds were also attracted to. Second, and even more important, humans burned off the prairie sod and chopped down the eastern forest. Now cowbirds could obtain all the food they needed without depending on those heavy hoofs to expose the soil. Instead of disappearing as the bison did, the cowbird population exploded, and cowbirds spread throughout the entire country to places where birds had never before encountered them. Some birds that were already low in numbers, like Kirtland's Warbler, became endangered. Right now, extensive cowbird trapping programs are crucial to protect from extinction endangered birds such as Kirtland's Warblers, Black-capped Vireos, and some populations of Bell's Vireos.

Birds that nest two or three times a season, such as Song and Chipping Sparrows, don't suffer population problems from cowbirds. Even if they lose a whole brood, they can raise enough babies in other broods that year to maintain the species. But *neotropical migrants*—those birds that winter in the New World tropics of Central and South America—get only one chance at nesting each year. They don't arrive back in the northwoods until late May or early June and are already headed south by early August. Cowbirds seriously compromise their ability to maintain their species.

Cowbirds are not forest birds—they live in open areas and edges, seldom entering a forest deeper than about 150 feet from the edge. Forests that remain contiguous are the last holdouts for healthy populations of some flycatchers, warblers, vireos, and tanagers. As we fragment the forest, we open up more and more edges for invasion by cowbirds and other opportunistic predators like crows, jays, foxes, raccoons, and coyotes.

On a birding trip to Arizona, I saw many warblers feeding baby cowbirds. It made me sad to think that Painted Redstarts and Grace's Warblers and other precious jewels may be harder for next year's birders to find thanks to these tenacious, ever-expanding parasites. When I discover a cowbird egg in a nest, I toss it out without a second thought—unless there are children present. I know birders who, upon finding a hatched baby cowbird in a nest, throw it on the ground and stomp on it. Even though I sympathize with their frustration and anger about the cowbird problem, I simply could not bring myself to do that, and I trust that no caring adult would do such a thing in front of children. The littlest humans understand something about vulnerability, and a nestling is hardly responsible for the "sins" of its species. When it comes right down to it, the "sinful" nature of the cowbird problem originated with humans anyway—the buffalo-bird brood parasitism system worked just fine for everyone until white settlers entered the equation.

Dealing with adult cowbirds is another issue. My own children have observed cowbird trapping operations at a Kirtland's Warbler nest area in Michigan. They were sad that so many birds were going to die (the cowbirds are painlessly euthanized with carbon monoxide), but they understood in their minds and accepted in their hearts that this is a tragic but important way of protecting a rare species.

The difficulty with many conservation issues is their complexity—it takes a careful weighing of all facets of an issue to come to a sensible and honorable solution, and there really may not be a satisfying end result for some troubling issues. To make information understandable, we often must simplify it by breaking down complex ideas or issues into their basic components. But to distort or leave out whole components from the equation because we dislike facing them is not simplification—it's propaganda. We must be fair when we discuss controversial issues, but fairness does not demand that we squelch our point of view. Fairness does not demand that we soften our outrage when the world we love is in jeopardy.

## Specific ways that children can help birds

The first birds children want to help are usually individuals rather than whole populations. Many wildlife biologists and managers emphasize the importance of populations and dismiss projects geared toward individual animals, but this is shortsighted, ignores our responsibilities as stewards of the planet, and is sometimes foolish—after all, whole populations are made

## Growing love

Human concerns about others grow from our love for our immediate family and friends to our community, our state, and our nation, ultimately encompassing the whole world. So too does our love for the environment often begin with our love for an individual creature, grow to encompass our love for the plants and animals that nurture it, and blossom into love and concern for a whole ecosystem.

up of individuals. The more endangered a local population is, the more valuable and even critical each individual becomes. And the more experience people gain in treating common species, the more knowledgeable we are when rarer birds need help. Most of the birds treated at rehabilitation centers are injured by cars, cats, picture windows, wires, poisons, or shotguns. We bear some responsibility as moral creatures to at least try to correct the damage we inflict on our world and the creatures that share it with us. And, most importantly, when a child helps an individual bird in trouble, the experience may foster and nurture the love that child feels toward the whole species, making it more likely that in the future he or she will learn about broader issues involving that species and care enough to ultimately work to protect the whole population.

## Injured birds

It is illegal for kids to raise wild baby birds or even to help injured birds beyond bringing them to rehabilitation centers. This is usually for the best—after all, it takes experience and knowledge to keep a bird alive, and children may be overwhelmed with sadness when a bird they're trying to help dies anyway.

But when they find a baby or hurt bird, kids need to know what to do right away. Three middle-school girls in my town, home alone one Friday evening, were playing in their backyard when a little falcon ripped through the yard right smack into their hammock, getting hopelessly tangled. These were resourceful, logical girls. First they called our local humane society and the zoo but got recorded messages. Then they called the local conservation officer who told them to "let nature take its course." Few children would be willing to let nature take its course right there in their hammock, so these girls did what kids nowadays do when they're *really* in trouble—they called 911. The state patrol dispatcher had my name as a licensed bird rehabilitator and put me onto the case.

Meanwhile, one of the girls, despairing that any grown-up

was ever going to help, took matters into her own hands. She looked up the bird in the field guide and discovered that it was a Merlin. These little falcons have treacherous talons, so she put on her mom's gardening gloves and extricated it from the hammock. This was tricky—in its struggles the bird had twisted one wing entirely around, and she was scared she'd break the wing bones. But she was gentle, patient, and careful, and she managed just fine. When she had unhooked the little predator, she straightened out its twisted wing as best she could. She didn't want to stress it by keeping it in her hands, so she considered what to do next. It seemed to her that a hurt, scared bird might be better off in the dark, so she placed it in a cardboard box and covered it. By the time I arrived, the work was done—all I had to do was bring it to a raptor specialist. She had done such an excellent job that, although the wing muscle was torn, the bone was unbroken, and the bird healed perfectly. These girls were proud of themselves. They did a perfect job.

Normally I would advise against children handling any raptor—this is a job for a grown-up wearing very thick gloves because all hawks and owls have dangerous talons. And injured birds of any kind must be handled gently but firmly, which the smallest children aren't good at (but, then again, neither are inexperienced grown-ups). To catch a grounded and clearly injured bird, try dropping a pillowcase or lightweight towel over it. Injured birds are often in shock. It's a good idea to dribble some Gatorade or Pedialyte into an injured bird's mouth to restore its electrolytes. Then do exactly as those girls did: place it in a small, dark cardboard box and call the nearest rehabilitator, nature center, or state or federal wildlife specialist to ask if they can take the bird or advise you where to bring it.

## Baby birds

Children seem to be baby-bird magnets, finding them everywhere, and they always seem to think that the baby birds need them. But most baby birds are much safer left alone. I include the following instructions partly to show why it's so difficult to raise baby birds successfully (in hopes of discouraging people who want to do it for fun or to give kids a novel experience), and partly because if you do find yourself temporarily saddled with a baby bird, I want both you and the bird to survive the ordeal not too much worse for the wear.

There are two kinds of baby songbirds: *nestlings* and *fledglings*. Nestlings are those that have fallen or been tossed from their nest. If you find one, do your darnedest to get it back in the nest. Don't worry about handling it (gently, of course!)— birds, like humans, recognize babies by sight or sound, not by smell. As long as you put it back in the right nest, the parents will not reject it.

Fledglings are the toddlers of the bird world. Just as toddler humans get bored in their cribs and learn to climb out, fledgling songbirds don't want to stay put in a boring little nest, so they jump out. They hop around testing their wings, tasting bugs, and checking out the big world. When hungry, they make high-pitched little notes that their parents can hear from a fairly long distance. Problem is, those parents have three or four other little toddlers hopping about, too—they may be too busy with the others to respond to one baby for quite some time.

If you're dealing with a fledgling, you needn't bother putting it back in the nest because it won't stay there. If it's in a safe place where no cats, dogs, or crows are hanging around, either leave it entirely alone or pick it up and set it gently in a tree or bush where predators are less likely to find it.

What should you do if you can't get a nestling back in its nest or if you're absolutely certain that the parents are dead? Then try to find a licensed rehabilitator or a nature center that can take it. But, meanwhile, you need to keep it alive. Keep a nestling in an ice cream bucket lined with paper towels. Wadding up toilet paper to form a nest inside makes cleanup quick and easy. (And keep it meticulously clean!) You can temporarily keep fledglings (any baby birds that won't stay put in an ice cream bucket) in a fairly large cardboard box. Don't ever put them in a cage—the metal bars will fray their flight feathers.

Baby birds have a very rapid metabolic rate to match their growth. It takes only fourteen to eighteen days for a baby Blue Jay to grow from tiny egg size to full adult weight. This requires a lot of protein. So what do you feed it? Not worms. Robins do feed their babies many worms but only in addition to a wide variety of insects and berries. Most other songbirds feed their babies many kinds of insects. True finches such as Pine Siskins, American Goldfinches, Purple and House Finches, and Evening Grosbeaks feed their babies regurgitated seed. How are you going to know what the best diet is for your bird? It's very hard—that's why the parent bird is more qualified to raise the baby. None of us can possibly find the exact variety and balance of foods that a natural parent bird would.

Mealworms are the best single food for most baby songbirds (except true finches). I keep mealworms year-round, but most people don't usually have them handy. For a temporary substitute (to be used for no more than a day or two) that will work well with most species, you can make up a batch of what I call "gloppity glop." This is the basic recipe:

2 cups high-protein dog food (dry)

1 package Knox gelatin

1/4 cup applesauce

boiling water

Grind up the dog food in a blender. Pour into a bowl and mix with dry gelatin. Add applesauce. Stir as you add boiling water little by little until you end up with a mixture the consistency of wet cookie dough. Put the glop in margarine containers and freeze.

After gloppity glop freezes and then thaws, it's a fine consistency for feeding baby birds, but it's far from a complete diet—it's missing critical vitamins and minerals essential for growth and maintenance. I add drops of liquid bird vitamins (with vitamin D3) whenever I feed baby birds—I don't add the vitamins when I prepare the food mixture because boiling breaks down vitamins. Without vitamins, growing bones will be deformed. I also add a tablespoon of Avimin (a mineral supplement) to my recipe along with a baby-bird hand-feeding mixture available at pet shops. I also give baby birds plenty of mealworms. Robins, waxwings, and jays also need fruit. I feed true finches a hand-feeding mix developed for baby cockatiels and budgies—that's a good substitute for regurgitated seeds.

I never use forceps or a toothpick to feed babies—it's too easy to hurt their soft mouths. Instead, I use my fingers to wad the food up into a pea-sized blob, and then I put it in the mouth with two fingers and help it down the throat a bit with my pinkie. Babies should be fed every fifteen or twenty minutes during most of the day, but if meals are generous, you can take a break for an hour or so now and then. Songbirds never feed their babies after dark, allowing parents to get a good night's sleep, but you have to start feeding them again as soon as it gets light.

It's complicated teaching a baby bird to become wild. As soon as they recognize the sound of me whistling, I keep all my fledglings loose outdoors for much of the day. They don't need to learn how to take off and land from coffee tables and sofas to survive in the real world—they need practice hopping and flying in trees and bushes. Real parent birds teach their babies how to find and obtain natural food, though most babies can eventually figure it out on their own. But as a foundling learns, which takes weeks or even months (much longer than if they'd had their parents' help), they need someone to keep feeding them, or they will starve. Keeping track of them is hard work. If you raise a baby bird successfully indoors and then simply let it go, the bird will die a slow death of starvation.

For more information about helping injured or orphaned birds, see *Care of the Wild, Feathered and Furred,* by Mae Hickman and Maxine Guy. If you're really interested, and have the time and space to consider becoming a licensed rehabilitator yourself, consider a membership in the National Wildlife Rehabilitator's Association—consult your library for a current address.

Some children with strong empathy and compassion are good at rehabilitation. If they are old enough to meet the requirements, encourage them to volunteer as helpers in a local zoo, rehab facility, or nature center. Some of the children in my neighborhood help me by catching moths and other insects to feed my charges. Kids who, like me, are reluctant to kill insects sometimes pick them off car grills.

## Other ways kids can help birds

Planting bird-friendly trees and shrubs and constructing and setting out feeders, nest boxes, and nesting materials are wonderful, positive ways of helping individual birds. But be careful not to encourage introduced species, brood parasites, and opportunistic nest predators like crows and jays any more than necessary. House Sparrows and European Starlings that are well-fed are likely to have more babies than those that have to scrounge for food. If cowbirds turn up at your feeder, shut it down for a few days. All of these species get plenty enough help from humans.

If you have a picture window that birds frequently fly against, hang netting or strips of colorful cloth to the upper window frame, or cut out silhouettes of hawks to tape to the window. I used to have a killer picture window, but haven't had a single bird smack into it since my husband and kids built a feeder right onto the window frame—apparently as they feed there, birds notice the glass more easily.

Some things that families do may hurt birds. Show kids you care about birds by keeping cats indoors and never using lawn pesticides. The best solution for weeds is to pull them. If you hate dandelions so much that you really want to put poison on your lawn, at least minimize the toxicity by spot spraying individual weeds rather than spraying the whole lawn.

**Chemical-free lawn care**
- Mow high, leaving grass 3 inches tall
- Don't rake new clippings
- Don't mow when the weather is hot and dry
- Don't water unless absolutely necessary
- Water only early in the morning
- Seed lawn in fall
- If you must fertilize, do so only in fall, using one pound or less of nitrogen for every 1,000 square feet.

**Keep birds alive: drive 55**

Millions of birds are killed on highways every year. As soon as you notice a bird (or mammal) on the road ahead, especially in traffic where you can't slow down much, gently beep your horn—the warning may save its life. The slower you drive, the better chance birds have of noticing your approach. Driving slow helps birds in another way, too—cars going 55 get far better gas mileage than those going 65, and those going 45 do even better! Saving energy helps the environment for both humans and birds and maintains future energy reserves for our children as well.

Encourage neighbors to stop using lawn sprays, some of which contain insecticides as well as herbicides. Children might even offer to pull the weeds for a fair price. Weed-pulling makes a fine service project for Brownies and Cub Scouts. If you golf or belong to a country club, perhaps you and the children can encourage the managers to reduce or eliminate pesticide use.

Everything we do to improve the environment will also help birds. The enormous energy consumption of humans on a heavily-burdened planet takes an enormous toll on birds: mining processes poison water, dams destroy natural wetlands, power lines and wind turbines directly kill flying birds. Ironically, one energy source that kills very few birds directly or indirectly on a day-to-day basis, nuclear power, has the potential for serious destruction, with storage of spent radioactive fuel an unresolved issue and overall safety of plants an ever-present, serious consideration. Turning unnecessary lights off and other small ways that children and their families conserve energy are "drops in the bucket" but still positive actions that really do help birds. Slowing down our driving speed both conserves energy *and* reduces roadkills.

Writing letters to the editor is a popular assignment in some classes, but few newspapers publish letters by kids, so encourage them to put their letter-writing energy to other uses as well. If an issue is of national importance, they might write to their senator and representative in Congress. Help them with research so their letter is informed and proposes positive solutions.

State laws and, once in a while, local ordinances are proposed that affect birds. Letters to state legislators or city council members may make a real difference. Again, the more informed an opinion is, the more seriously it will be taken. Local conservation organizations can keep you up-to-date on local and state issues. Greenberg and Reiser's *Bring Back the Birds* has excellent selections on letter writing and citizen action that can be adapted for children.

When children discover or learn of a local hazard that hurts birds, documenting and publicizing the problem can make grown-ups take notice so that sometimes they'll do something to solve the problem. Photographing dead birds—washed ashore in polluted water, fallen beneath buildings or towers, or simply killed by a neighbor's cat—may help persuade people to change harmful practices.

## Counting birds

We usually need to prove serious declines in whole animal populations in order to influence large changes. The most useful information comes from census data taken over long periods of time. Involvement in Cornell University's Project Feeder-Watch or Project PigeonWatch is an excellent introduction to data-keeping, and participants make a genuine contribution to ornithological research. Children are welcome to participate in both projects, individually or in groups. (For more information, see Chapter 2.)

The Christmas Bird Count, sponsored by the National Audubon Society, also collects long-term data, which some scientists use for studying population trends. Motivated children are welcome to participate in most counts. Contact your local or state bird club for more information. There is a small participation fee.

Some states conduct Breeding Bird Atlas projects, wherein they gather data to determine exactly which birds nest in exactly which areas of the state. Older, highly motivated children might work with an experienced adult partner to survey an area for this kind of project. For more information, contact your local or state bird club.

One of the most important long-term censuses is the Breeding Bird Survey, coordinated by the United States Fish and Wildlife Service. You must be an expert on bird identification to participate in this, but if an older child is serious about birds and getting skilled at identifying them, and if a Breeding Bird Survey counter needs an assistant for recording data, perhaps

**Local bird counts**

Many newspapers cover local Christmas Bird Counts, printing information about how to participate. Other ways to hook up with your local count include calling a local bird club or getting hold of the latest Christmas Bird Count issue of *Audubon Field Notes* (usually number 4 of each volume— if it isn't in your library, you should be able to get it through interlibrary loan). Look through the counts listed for your state. Each listing includes the name and address of the count compiler, who is the person to contact. Teachers and students are often assigned to areas where they can expect to see many common birds.

**Book of hope**

*Nights of the Pufflings*, by Bruce McMillan, is a lovely book about how real children save thousands of baby puffins every year. The author's extraordinary photography, simple, elegant prose, magical sense of wonder, and powerful conservation ethic combine to produce a book of love and hope without sad and fearful warnings or preachy lessons. This book is appropriate for preschoolers, yet adults and even high schoolers will enjoy it.

you can help arrange a match. Contact your local or state bird club to find out if a survey route is in your area.

Many kids worry about the tropical rain forest. Help them grow familiar with the birds of Central and South America. The Internet is rapidly becoming the place to study tropical issues—some on-line groups follow migrating birds from one place to another. In early 1996, the Internet was the main source of information about a tragic die-off of tens of thousands of Swainson's Hawks killed by pesticides in South America.

You don't need to be on the information superhighway to exchange information with people from other areas or other countries. If your children correspond with foreign pen pals, perhaps you can trade an American field guide for one of theirs. Virtually every bird book includes scientific as well as common names—children can look through a foreign bird book for species that look familiar and try to match them with related species in American bird books. It's especially fun to look through bird books from countries that use a different alphabet—scientific names stick out wonderfully because they're always written in Latin. Some birds from far away are identical to our American birds—comparing scientific names will reveal which ones.

Some conservation organizations are specifically involved in international bird preservation—interested children might save up their money to join one. The International Council for Bird Preservation, The Nature Conservancy, Conservation International, Natural Resources Defense Council, Wildlife Conservation International, and World Wildlife Fund are all worthwhile. *International Wildlife*, published by the National Wildlife Federation, and *National Geographic* are perhaps the most readable magazines about international conservation issues.

## Unless someone cares

What children love, they love with intensity, and when something they love is in trouble, they want desperately to help it. If they don't know how to help, they may feel overwhelmed by powerlessness.

My daughter, Katie, saw her first Passenger Pigeons when she was five years old. Of course they were dead, housed in a museum showcase. Reading the display signs, she learned that millions of these beautiful doves with their rosy feathers filled the skies long before her grandparents were born, but people killed every one of them. Katie cried out of heartfelt sadness that every single Passenger Pigeon was dead, frustration and loss that she would never, ever be able to see one, and anger that people long ago were so selfish. I didn't have the heart to tell her about the Spotted Owl controversy raging right then in Oregon, where cars sported ugly bumper stickers showing barbecued owls. It's hard enough for children to face the issues of declining species without learning too much about the cruelty and selfishness of our own species.

Margaret Mead said, "Never doubt that a small group of thoughtful, committed citizens can change the world. Indeed, it is the only thing that ever has." Sometimes the world is changed by revolutions, with the blood, upheaval, and sorrow that revolutions exact. We parents and teachers have the power to change the world in more gentle fashion but only if we make a conscious decision to do so.

As Dr. Seuss said in *The Lorax*, "UNLESS someone like you cares a whole awful lot, Nothing is going to get better. It's not."

# APPENDIX I

# THE WRITE STUFF

**B**ird study involves keeping records of the birds we see, where we see them, and what they're doing. In this appendix, you will find several effective methods for recording this information. At some point, your kids may need to write a report, either for science class or science and language arts both. Writing a report about a bird is one of the requirements for the Boy Scout Bird Study Merit Badge. Procedures for researching and writing such a report are also included in this appendix.

## Field notebooks

Field notebooks can be a valuable repository of hard data, interesting facts, and treasured memories, but children tend to be great minimalists before they grasp the point to them. Families can list from memory (aided by a checklist) the birds they saw on an outing, taking time on the way home or before bed to jot down memories of the most fun and most beautiful or exciting birds or events of the day, but scout leaders and teachers usually want kids to get into the good habit of keeping an actual field notebook.

The first field notebook can be a loose-leaf binder or just pages stapled together. This way you can prepare simple data sheets for the kids to fill out. For every trip, long or short, kids should record date, time, and location. A complete list of species seen is a good idea. Especially for small children, it's simplest to put a short checklist of the most likely species on the data sheet. They can check off the listed birds as they see them, so all they need to actually write is names of additional species at the bottom.

Little children don't understand the concept of habitat—it's enough at first to note whether you're birding from a playground, park, or sidewalk. As children get older and learn more about plants and animals and their interactions, they will grow ever more sophisticated about habitat, progressing from "park" to "woods" to "deciduous woods" to "20-acre beech-maple woodlot bordering open lawn of urban park." At any stage, taping a few leaves into their notebooks can not only provide a useful record of the habitat visited, it can also weave into children's minds a connection between birds and the plants they need.

Serious adult birders make notes about and sometimes draw sketches of the plumages of unfamiliar and rare birds they see. If you set aside an area of a data sheet for descriptions and/or sketches, children can practice this important skill as well as identification.

As children grow in knowledge, data sheets can become more complex, incorporating behavior studies as well as descriptions.

Data sheets will get wrinkled and torn unless protected. A clipboard is well designed for this job, but if you can't afford clipboards for everyone, you might improvise by securing data sheets to stiff cardboard with clothespins. Even so, data sheets will certainly get creased and torn. As a teacher, my only requirement about the appearance of field notebooks was that they be legible.

Scientists use indelible ink to record data, which makes losing or altering data difficult. That isn't an important issue with elementary children, especially compared to the issue of legibility. I'd encourage or even require kids to use pencils until they're at least in junior high and would require even high-schoolers to bring pencils for drawing birds.

You can design your data sheets with space for recording the whimsical elements of bird adventures or restrict the use of field notebooks and data sheets to scientific data and give other opportunities for journal-keeping. As a bird study program grows to include behavior and natural history, data sheets will grow, and field notebooks will become ever more interesting and detailed.

## Reports

When you're a little child, there's a lot of work involved in writing even a couple of sentences. Dictating stories and reports for adults to transcribe is an excellent first lesson in report writing. Many older children have difficulties with or dislike the physical act of writing. Once they master typing skills, a computer is a wonderful aid, but until then, a keyboard is just as daunting as pen and paper. To take some of the pressure off children with these problems, occasionally allow even big kids to dictate their stories to an adult "secretary." This serves as a powerful reminder that writing is little more than well-thought-out speech.

## Researching reports

Many children don't go beyond an encyclopedia when researching reports, sometimes because it's an easy way to avoid hard work and sometimes because they really don't know where else to look. Help them explore other possibilities. The best single source for an enormous wealth of bird information is John K. Terres's *The Audubon Encyclopedia of North American Birds.* No school library should be without it. Also look for magazine articles (many are indexed in *The Reader's Guide to Periodical Literature)* and other books. The Dewey decimal system catalogs bird books under 598—browse through both the children's and adult nonfiction sections of a library to uncover unexpected treasures. Don't insist that kids stick to books for their grade level. High school students may find wonderfully interesting facts in picture books or "first books," and kinder-gartners can often clearly understand the pictures and some written information in the most sophisticated adult bird books. In Appendix III you will find basic bird references that include facts about almost every species in North America.

When I'm writing about a specific bird, I often look it up in the index of various college ornithology textbooks, which are available in libraries. Even old editions have lots of great facts. That's how I found out that a Tundra Swan has 25,216 feathers compared to a Ruby-throated Hummingbird's 940 and that the Black-capped Chickadee's normal body temperature is about 106 degrees during daytime but drops down to as low as 86 degrees on cold nights. These are the kinds of trivia that can spice up a report and ignite excitement and interest at the same time.

To discourage copying material I used two strategies. Sometimes I ask the children to read an article or book all the way through and then close it and write down on index cards each fact they remember—these are usually the most memorable and interesting items. Just in case they forgot something important, I have them reread the article looking specifically for other interesting facts and double-checking the facts they've already recorded. These cards are easy to organize as they plan the body of their report. A paper cutter and used paper from my recycling bin make cheap "index cards."

At other times, I make a worksheet of twenty or thirty questions that their research about a bird should answer (such as the derivation of its name, any nicknames, its scientific name and meaning, description, length, weight, food, habitat, range, nesting habits, flight pattern, interesting behaviors, conservation problems, etc.). I tell the children to make their answers as short as possible, absolutely not using complete sentences. They are encouraged to cut up these worksheets and use them like index cards to organize their thoughts and plan the report.

Great reports include much more than mere factual information. To get their creative juices flowing, ask children about the first time they ever saw the bird they are studying, why they think it's a wonderful species, why they would love to see it in the wild, what life would be like if they turned into that bird, etc. Have them develop a list of adjectives and verbs that apply to the bird's appearance and behavior. Come up with appropriate alliterative descriptions and phrases such as loon lullabies, vulture vomit, and cute coots with their white snoots. A little creativity can transform even a dry subject into something enticingly interesting. Once, for a college physiology class, I wrote a paper about bird digestion titled "Alimentary, My Dear Hoatzin."

If children remember reading poems or stories about their bird, perhaps they can find one or two interesting short passages to quote. Ogden Nash and Emily Dickenson both wrote many poems about birds—check collections of their poetry for interesting possibilities. Show older children how to use *Bartlett's Familiar Quotations*, which has wonderful quotes about such species as the eagle, owl, osprey, jay, bluebird, and crow.

Has this bird been designated as an official state bird? If so, how did the state come to choose it? Is it pictured on a postage stamp? Does it serve as symbol of a sports team? Is it used to illustrate greeting cards? Is there a cartoon bird patterned after it? Do they know any jokes about it?

Is it a game bird? If so, do they know anyone who has hunted it? That person might have interesting stories and facts to uncover in an interview. I've even heard interesting tales about chickadees picking dried blood from shaving cuts of hunters sitting in their deer stands. Local bird-watchers may have exciting personal stories to relate. Might there be other sources to question? Ornithologists, bird rehabilitators, wildlife biologists, state natural resource department nongame specialists, and other professionals may enjoy being interviewed, especially if the child prepares interesting questions beforehand. Over years of teaching, you may collect lists of resource people and substantial amounts of report material from which children can draw information and ideas.

## Organizing the information

Once information is gathered, there's one more step before actually beginning to write. My job requires me to create three radio programs about birds every week along with writing newspaper and magazine articles on a regular basis, so I'm sort of a professional report writer. I never write anything until I have an "angle," with an opening that tells me where that story should lead. If children pretend that their report is going to be a magazine or newspaper story, sometimes they get a better sense of audience and how to engage their readers' interest. I always pretend my big brother is going to read everything I write. When I was little, he used to tell me that everything I said was "so stupid." Now I try to write things that would impress him or make him laugh. Many children have a similar figure in their life that may serve as an imaginary reader.

If you simply tell them to make the first sentence of their report what my own English teacher used to call a "topic sentence," it will almost definitely be an uninspired line that might as well have come from an encyclopedia. Instead, have the children read through the material they've gathered and use their imaginations to come up with an opening sentence. It could be a joke; a brief story about some personal encounter with a bird; a beautiful, funny, sad, or exciting original sentence or quote; or any item of information that grabs a reader.

An easy approach with younger students is to give them a thesis to defend, such as: "The most amazing (or the silliest, or most interesting, or most bizarre) bird in the universe is X because . . . "

Once they have an angle, kids can work out a reasonable way to organize the facts they've collected. Point out that even something as seemingly dry as a scientific name may be interesting. The generic name of the Turkey Vulture is *Cathartes*, which comes from Greek and means "purifier." This name was inspired either from the vulture's diet (it purifies the landscape by eating, and thus removing, rotten, dead animals) or from its habit of vomiting on predators when cornered (cathartics clear the digestive system.) *Tyrannus tyrannus*, the Eastern Kingbird, is a feisty little bird, the "tyrant of tyrants," which, if it had lived 65 million years ago, probably would have dive-bombed any *Tyrannosaurus rex* that dared approach its nest.

Encourage kids to weave facts together in different ways, sometimes as questions (Did you know . . . ?), sometimes as explanations of more fanciful material (e.g. "Quoth the raven, 'Nevermore!'" Edgar Allan Poe wrote this poem about a bird that really can talk . . .).

The best final sentences never just trail off—they leave the reader satisfied that the report is complete and often end in a strong, evocative noun. Readers respond emotionally to good endings. The easiest to write are humorous, but sometimes a report is written to make the reader feel sad about an endangered bird or hopeful that a bird that had problems may be coming back or delighted by a pleasing or silly image. A report about ravens may end with the word "Nevermore!"

### Other kinds of reports

Research papers may be written in many styles other than typical nonfiction "reports." Children may develop a field guide of birds they've seen, using photocopied black-and-white drawings or their own illustrations. Or they can keep a phenology notebook, including their own or the whole class's observations along with information gleaned from references. Children may write to a company regarding a bird-related product or voice their concerns about a pertinent issue, or request bird-related information from an ornithologist.

For fun, offer kids some of the following suggestions: set reports in rhyme. Write a biography of a fictitious individual bird, developing the story line from birth through the bird's prime, including several adventures that could really happen. An autobiography (told, of course, from the bird's point of view) is another interesting approach. How about a commercial to "sell" your bird or a political message to persuade viewers to vote for it? Try writing a script for a TV movie with an interesting plot line, incorporating facts into the stage directions, set description, action, and dialog. Write commercials to go along with the TV script, selling products to birds (like Jaybelline Eye Cosmetics or bulletproof vests for ducks and geese). Create and write a detailed description of an imaginary video game in which your bird is either the hero or the villain and come up with foes and adventures based on your research.

## Scientific papers

As kids develop their written skills and master more complicated elements of bird study, they may begin writing scientific papers, perhaps describing an experiment or field study they have conducted. Most junior high students can understand papers published in state ornithological journals, and by high school, some students may be able to understand a few well-written papers in major ornithological journals. When you require students to write their own scientific papers, encourage them to strive for being understood rather than sounding profound.

Scientific papers should have a simple *title* clearly stating exactly what the point of the paper is, followed by an *abstract*— a very brief summary of what the project or experiment showed. Some kids are stymied by the whole idea of an abstract, since everything they say in it is repeated in the body of the paper. Explain that scientists read abstracts to efficiently learn about current research in many areas of ornithology, and read entire papers only when they are pertinent to their own research lines or hold some other attraction.

The *introduction* of a scientific paper should include

background information necessary for explaining the point behind the project; the *materials and methods* section explains exactly how the experiment or project was carried out; the *results* section presents the data collected plus pertinent observations; the *discussion* interprets the data; and the *conclusions* makes clear statements about what the child learned or discovered by doing the project and whether there are any broader implications of the study. For example, if a child was comparing the number of robin nests in yards treated with pesticides versus untreated yards, he or she might make a recommendation about lawn-care treatments based on the results.

### Rewarding fine work

Providing blank bound books for a report or story may encourage the children's finest work. My son Tommy's third-grade teacher invited parents to attend an "Author's Day" on which the children displayed and read their finest work for us.

Encourage children to publish excellent work. Your class may compile a magazine or book about birds or natural history with a broad range of articles and illustrations. A school newspaper is a good first place to publish work outside the classroom. Local bird club newsletters may publish one or two short stories, poems, reports, or drawings on a "children's page." Some shops that sell bird feed also publish newsletters and may be interested in including high-quality work by area children. A local or regional newspaper may publish well-written and well-researched letters by children about issues such as cat leash-laws and the use of herbicides and insecticides on lawns. A few nationally distributed children's magazines publish work by kids, but the probability of any given student being published in one of these is remote.

Whether or not reports are publishable, as you read them, find a variety of ways to affirm good work. Comments like "You sure explained that well," "What a great line—I wish I'd thought of that," "That made me laugh," and "Wow! I didn't know that!" encourage exactly the kinds of research, expressiveness, and creativity you're trying to foster. As a professional writer, I know how pleasurable it is to receive specific praise rather than a generic "Good job!" One of my friends marks lines of my manuscripts with "LOL"—her notation for items that made her "laugh out loud." She draws simple happy and sad faces or exclamation points near parts that made her respond emotionally. I never feel hurt or huffy when she criticizes a section or finds a mistake because she's lavish and specific with praise. I bet kids feel pretty much the same way.

# APPENDIX II

## SIMPLE
# GIFTS

Whether you teach bird study in a formal school setting or at home with preschoolers, fun and simple projects may serve as appealing introductions or special activities to reinforce learning. The projects in this chapter were easy ways for some of my friends and me to share our interest in birds with adults and children, and they will be easy ways for children to share their interest in birds with others.

### The trickster's field guide pouch

Raven is the trickster of the Pacific Northwest who's always getting into trouble. One time Raven stole fresh water and, in his hurry to escape, spilled drops that formed the earth's rivers and lakes. Another time, Raven disguised himself as a deer and stole fire, which he carried on his tail. When the Fire Owner discovered him, Raven hid in the forest and accidentally set the trees on fire. Ever since then, people have been able to use fire, thanks to Raven's naughty mistake.

Raven once got so bored in the World of Darkness that he made a hole in the clouds and flew to the Sky-World, where he changed himself to a leaf floating in the water. When the Sky-Chief's daughter took a drink, she swallowed this leaf and magically had a baby boy. But the baby was really Raven! He cried and begged to play with a box containing the sun until his grandfather, the Sky-Chief, finally gave in. Off Raven flew with it through a hole in the clouds and back to earth, which was now no longer the world of darkness.

Once Raven sneaked into a bird-watcher's pocket to peek at a field guide. Birds from far and near came to laugh at him, so the bird-watcher saw many beautiful species.

This Raven field guide pouch is a gift that two of my friends, Joan Hinds and Jean Becker, designed for you. Their company, Fancywork and Fashion, publishes sewing pattern books for 18" vinyl and porcelain dolls. Jean and Joan hope that your Raven pouch will attract many exciting birds to you.

**Raven field guide pouch**

This is a good project for an adult and a youngster to work on together. The result—besides rewarding your creative souls—is a waterproof field-guide-sized pocket you can hang from your belt. It requires only a little machine sewing. The raven is ironed on and embellished with fabric paint.

## Supplies

- Two 8" x 23" rectangles of Ultrex, a breathable, waterproof fabric (we used one rectangle of brick red for the outside and one rectangle of black for the lining)
- One 4" x 6" rectangle of black Ultrex for the raven
- One 4" x 6" piece of Aleene's or other brand fusible web
- One bottle of Scribbles or other brand teal-colored fabric paint
- Two sew-on Velcro dots
- matching sewing thread

Notes: Seam allowances are $1/2$". Set the stitch length on your sewing machine a little longer than usual to reduce the number of needle holes; pin sparingly, and only in the seam allowances. Every time you pierce the fabric the waterproofing is compromised.

# RAVEN PATTERN

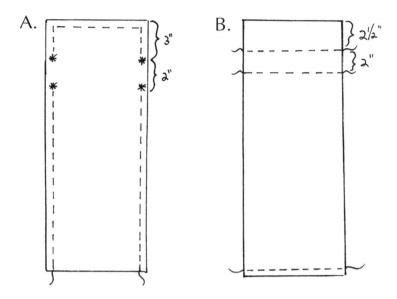

## Instructions

1. Place the two rectangles of fabric right sides together. Pin together at the top and bottom. Measure down 3" from the top on each side and mark as shown by the asterisks in illustration A. Measure down another 2" and mark those two points.

2. Stitch along the dotted lines shown in illustration A. Do not sew where there are no dotted lines between the two pencil lines and at the bottom of the rectangle. Cut away some of the corners to reduce bulk. Turn right side out and press with medium (not too hot!) iron.

3. Fold in the fabric $^1/2$" at the open end, pin and topstitch across, about $^3/8$" from the folded-in edge. Turn the pocket over so that you are looking at the side of the fabric which will be the lining of the pocket. Measure down $2^1/2$" from the top edge and draw a light pencil line across. Measure down another 2" and draw another line. Stitch along these lines to form the belt casing. See illustration B.

C.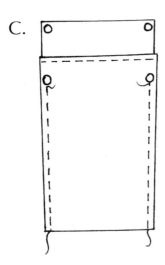

4. With the lining (in our case, the black fabric) on the inside, fold the rectangle up from the bottom so that the end you topstitched meets the top casing line. Pin the sides together and stitch $3/8$" from the edges as shown, starting at the bottom casing line. Leave the sides unstitched above that point so that the belt casing remains open. See illustration C.

5. Machine stitch the loopy halves of the Velcro dots at the top of the side stitching. Sew the fuzzy halves on the inside of the pocket flap as shown in illustration C.

6. Trace the outline only of the raven onto the bumpy side of the fusible web (the gluey side). Be sure that your lines are bold. Following manufacturer's instructions, use an iron to fuse the web to the wrong side of your raven fabric. Cut out the raven along the lines you will see through the web paper. Carefully remove the paper from the webbing.

7. Again following the manufacturer's instructions, center the raven on the pocket and iron it on. After it has cooled a minute, use the teal-colored fabric paint to freehand embellish the black raven as shown in the drawing. It's a really good idea to practice working with the paint on some scraps of fabric. Again, follow the manufacturer's instructions regarding drying time and cleanup. Slide your belt through the casing and buckle up!

© Fancywork and Fashion, 1996

## Origami cranes

Japanese law proclaims the graceful crane a "special natural monument." Cranes are long-lived birds that mate for life: in Japan, they are a symbol of happiness, longevity, and marital fidelity. Mated pairs perform courtship dances and songs, and their territorial calls can be heard up to two miles away. The Japanese expression *tsuru no hitokoe* ("the voice of the crane") refers to a tone of authority. We have two kinds of cranes in the United States: Sandhill and Whooping Cranes.

Origami is the Japanese traditional method of folding paper. I first learned how to fold paper when I was in college, and sometimes I made origami figures when I should have been studying for tests.

To make a paper crane, all you need is a 6" square piece of paper. Notebook paper and copy paper don't work well because they're too thick to make sharp creases. The dyes in genuine Japanese origami paper sometimes rub off on moist little fingers. I usually use wrapping paper, especially foil, which makes beautiful, shiny cranes. The paper needs to be perfectly square to work well—it's best to use a paper cutter, but scissors work well too. Use the back of the fingernail to make all creases sharp. With very little children and lower elementary kids, you might help make some of the folds.

**Origami crane**

# Directions for Folding Origami Crane

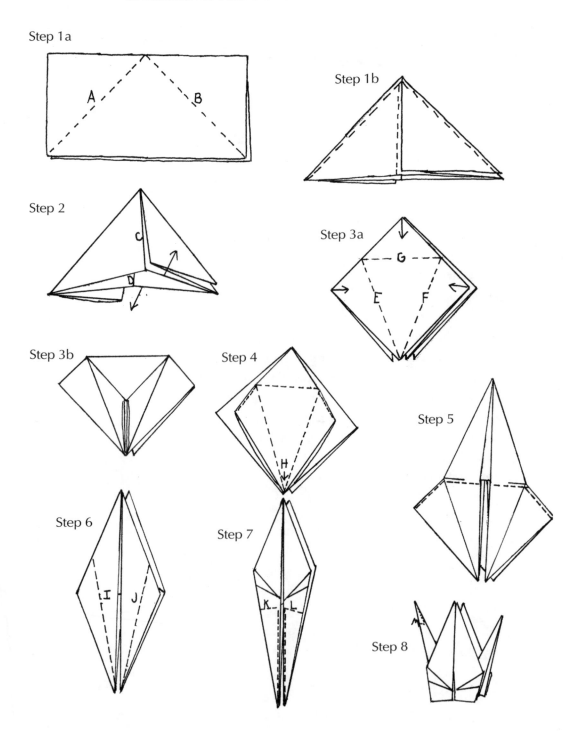

Step 1a

A    B

Step 1b

Step 2

C

D

Step 3a

G

E    F

Step 3b

Step 4

H

Step 5

Step 6

H    J

Step 7

K    L

Step 8

M

© Pfeifer-Hamilton Publishers  •  210 West Michigan  •  Duluth, MN 55810          (218) 727-0500

## Instructions

1. Fold your paper in half horizontally. Fold the top left corner away from you along line A. Fold the top right corner toward you along line B.

2. Open up the triangle like a paper hat and keep going. Crease on lines C and D to make a square. Put the open corners of the paper on the bottom.

3. Fold the top half of the paper along lines E, F, and G to crease it. Turn it over and crease the other side the same way.

4. Pull the top layer of paper up at point H, and using the creases to guide you, flatten into a diamond shape.

5. Turn over and repeat on the other side. Now you have a Crane Base. Many origami shapes begin with a Crane Base.

6. Half of the crane base is separated like legs. Point this half down. Fold the upper layer toward you along lines I and J. Turn it over and repeat.

7. Make sharp creases along lines K and L, folding both toward and away from you. Reverse fold (pulling up and tucking in) the tail and neck sections.

8. Make a crease along line M, and reverse fold (pulling up and tucking in) the head. Bend the wings down.

To display your crane, you can thread a long needle, make a big knot on one end of the thread, and push the needle through the crane from the bottom center through the point on the crane's back. Carefully pull the thread through, making sure to stop pulling before the knot reaches the top. Now you can pull the needle off the thread and tie a loop in the thread to use the crane as a hanging ornament. Or fashion several cranes into a mobile using straightened out paper clips, drinking straws, or backyard twigs to balance them.

My son Joey drew the illustrations for the crane project.

**Bird feeder plan**

Carrol Henderson, the supervisor of Minnesota's Non-Game Wildlife section of the Department of Natural Resources, shares feeding hints and a plan for a simple tray feeder from his book, *Wild About Birds: The D.N.R. Bird Feeding Guide.*

———

Tray feeders are among the most popular and adaptable of all bird feeders. They are very easy to make and should last a long time. One benefit of tray feeders is that they give birds a wide scope of vision, allowing them to feel relatively secure from predators. However, if tray feeders are placed too close to trees, bushes, or other obstacles, there is a danger of ambush by cats or raptors.

Almost any type of lumber or wood scraps can be used to create tray feeders. Some people even use a sheet of plywood on a stump or the top of a picnic table as a winter tray feeder.

Tray feeders should have some drain holes in the bottom and a cleaning gap on the side to make it easier to scrape out old or moldy seeds. It is better to regularly place smaller amounts of seeds in a tray feeder (no more than $1/4$" deep) than to fill it all the way to the top, which promotes the growth of mold and the germination of wet seeds. It also helps to stir up the seeds after a rain to help them dry out. Waste seeds under and around the feeder will need to be periodically cleaned up to avoid attracting mice, voles, or rats.

This small tray feeder is easy to build and easy to accommodate in small yards, on decks, or in garden areas. The feeder can be attached to the top of a stump, post, or pipe from one to five feet above the ground. The simplicity of the design makes it an excellent choice for small children to assemble.

The feeder may be used by a wide variety of common feeder birds such as chickadees, cardinals, Blue Jays, House Finches, Purple Finches, and grackles. Stock it with sunflower, safflower, corn, or millet mixes.

Due to territorial spacing, only a few birds will feed in a small space at the same time. For this reason you may want to have several of these feeders scattered around your garden, deck, or yard.

Remember that saw blades may take out $1/8$" of wood every time they cut a board. You must allow for the width of the saw blade when making your marks. Add that width to the length of each piece to be cut. Once you have cut out all the pieces, it's a good idea to assemble them by holding the pieces together and checking their fit. This is called a dry fit. You may need to do some minor trimming to get a tighter fit. Fasten with $1^5/8$" deck screws. You may predrill the holes with a $7/64$-inch drill bit.

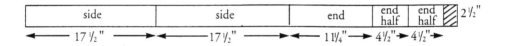

| side | side | end | end half | end half | 2½" |
|------|------|-----|----------|----------|-----|

← 17½" → ← 17½" → ← 11¼" → 4½" → 4½" →

\* This dimension assumes a $3/4$" thick board.
Sides should be $17^3/4$" if board is $7/8$" thick.

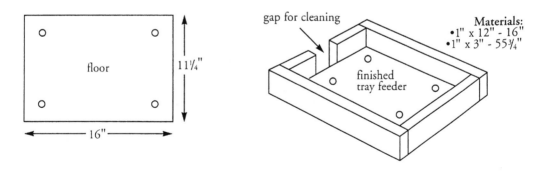

floor

11¼"

← 16" →

gap for cleaning

finished
tray feeder

Materials:
•1" x 12" - 16"
•1" x 3" - 55¾"

**Small tray feeder**

### Judy's bird

My good friend Judy Gibbs is a naturalist who teaches kids about birds. She designed a paper bird to show people how bird beaks and feet help them eat different foods and live in different habitats. My son Joey has modified the pattern for this book. Photocopy the drawings on pages 181 and 182, enlarging them if you like, and then cut out the pieces. Use paper fasteners to hook the various beaks to the face, feet to the belly, and tails to the rump, and you can "dial a bird."

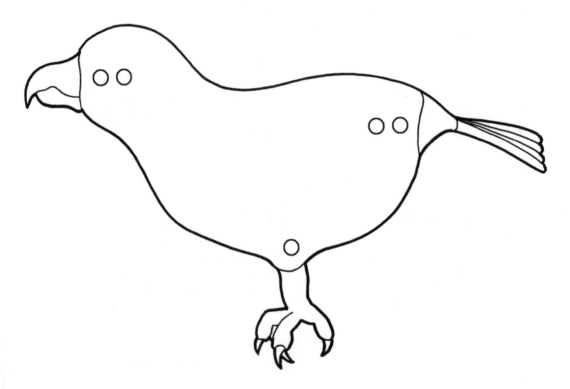

**Judy's bird example**

# Judy's Bird Feet and Tails

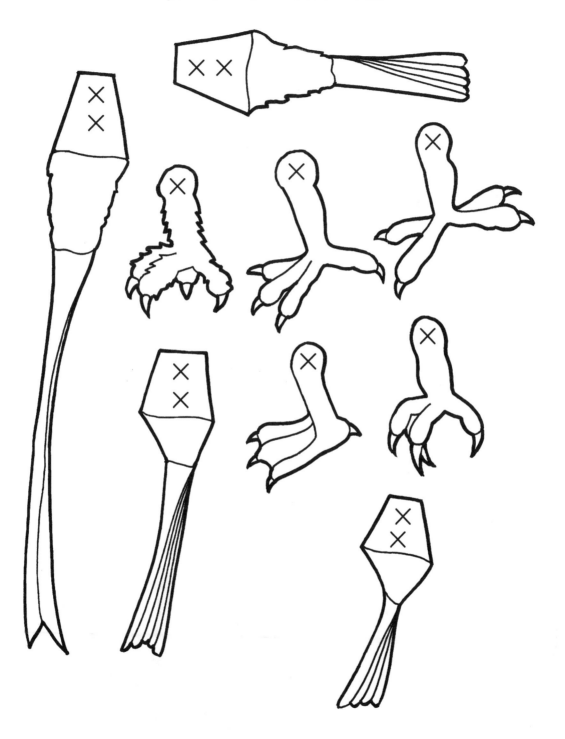

© Pfeifer-Hamilton Publishers • 210 West Michigan • Duluth, MN 55810     (218) 727-0500

# JUDY'S BIRD BODY AND BEAKS

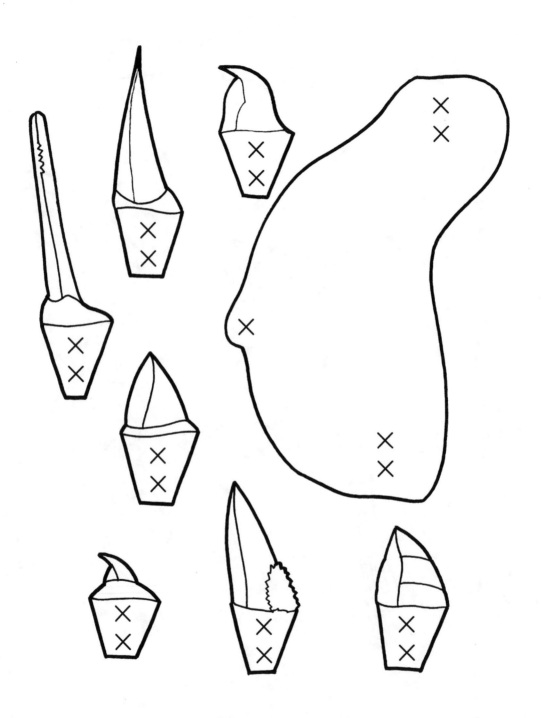

© Pfeifer-Hamilton Publishers • 210 West Michigan • Duluth, MN 55810          (218) 727-0500

# DRAWING BIRDS

Kathryn Marsaa, who illustrated this book, shared some ideas on how to draw a bird. Start with simple geometric shapes like ovals and triangles.

© Pfeifer-Hamilton Publishers • 210 West Michigan • Duluth, MN 55810          (218) 727-0500

# APPENDIX III

## ADDITIONAL
# BOOKS

If you can afford only one resource book besides a field guide, the book to have is John K. Terres's masterpiece, *The Audubon Society Encyclopedia of North American Birds* (Random House, New York, 1991). This enormous volume is the finest single reference book about birds available anywhere, with a treasury of information about every North American species and fascinating sections on just about every imaginable bird topic, all written in simple language. It has lavish black-and-white drawings of beaks, feet, skeletons, organ systems, and just about everything else, along with color photos of almost every North American bird species.

If children can read well enough to use a *World Book Encyclopedia*, they can use this book. Kids are especially impressed when they realize that this encyclopedia was not simply edited by Terres—he researched and wrote the entire 1,110-page volume himself. It cost $75 when originally published by Knopf in 1980 and was well worth it, but it now costs less than $40. Official names of some species have changed since publication, but this is still the single best resource there is. It's available at most public libraries.

### Bird behavior guides
A perfect set of resources for children of any age to begin bird behavior studies is Donald and Lillian Stokes's three-part series, *A Guide to the Behavior of Common Birds* (Little, Brown,

and Company, Boston, 1979). In these books, the authors carefully describe many of the specific behaviors of everyday birds, explain the contexts in which these behaviors are performed, and include a wealth of line drawings depicting various postures and displays. Many other books provide behavior information, including some facts that the Stokes leave out, but the Stokes's simple, straightforward approach makes these guides an excellent introduction to behavior study.

The book that I found most inspiring and helpful as a beginner, Joseph Hickey's *A Guide to Bird Watching* (Oxford University Press, London, 1943) is rather dated and above the reading and interest levels of most kids, but it's still an excellent book. The most useful part is the fifteen-page appendix article, "Outline for a Life-History Study," with questions that even little kids may want to explore. This book is available as a Dover Reprint and is still shelved at most public libraries.

**Books about ornithology and general bird biology**
David Burnie's *Eyewitness Books: Bird* (Alfred A. Knopf, New York, 1988) is a treasury of color photographs of bird feathers, eggs, nests, and skeletons that answers some of the common questions children ask about birds. It was supposedly written for children but is excellent for all ages.

*Zoobooks* (Wildlife Education Ltd., 9820 Willow Creek Road, Suite 300, San Diego, California 92131) are really eighteen-page magazines rather than books. Eight in the series are about birds: *Birds of Prey; Ducks, Geese & Swans; Eagles; Hummingbirds; Ostriches; Owls; Parrots;* and *Sea Birds.* The best feature is the full-color artwork. Each *Zoobook* has at least one drawing of a bird beneath its feathers, showing how the skeleton and muscles look.

Noble S. Proctor and Patrick J. Lynch's *Manual of Ornithology: Avian Structure and Function* (Yale University Press, New Haven, 1993), a beautiful book with lavishly illustrated black-and-white line drawings, explains virtually everything you could want to know about basic bird biology. Many of the drawings are suitable for even very small children, but the text, although straightforward and well-written, is for upper levels only.

Frank B. Gill's *Ornithology*, Second Edition (W. H. Freeman and Company, New York, 1994) is the standard college textbook for ornithology classes, but Gill's clear, easy-to-follow writing style makes this book worthwhile for people without a biology background. It is an excellent resource for any adult who wants a sense of what current ornithologists are researching and how they learn what they know. Motivated high school students will be able to understand most of the book.

Alexander Skutch, an ornithologist living in Costa Rica, had a problem with hummingbirds—they kept getting their tiny beaks caught in the wire mesh of his window screens, and if he didn't notice right away or wasn't home to rescue them, they often died. Many people would feel sad about such a hopeless situation, but Skutch did something about it—he took down all his window screens. Now birds fly right through his house, as do other creatures of the rain forest. Perhaps learning this is what turned me into a Skutch fan. He's written many wonderful books, such as *The Minds of Birds* (Texas A & M University Press, 1996), *Birds Asleep* (University of Texas Press, 1989), and *Parent Birds and Their Young* (University of Texas Press, 1976). Skutch's *The Life of the Woodpecker* (Ibis Publishing Company, 1985) and *The Life of the Hummingbird* (Crown Publishers, 1973) are classics. These are all technical books, so understanding them will be a stretch for middle schoolers and even high school students, but they're so interesting that motivated kids will be richly rewarded.

**Books about conservation**

Most people realize that many birds are in trouble, but few people understand why. We can get a handle on this sad but complicated subject with John Terborgh's *Where Have All the*

*Birds Gone?* (Princeton University Press, 1989). The birds facing the biggest problems are migrants that winter in the tropics. Richard M. DeGraaf and John H. Rappole's *Neotropical Migratory Birds: Natural History, Distribution, and Population Changes* (Comstock Publishing Associates, 1995) is limited to these species. These books are both written in technical language, more for college than high school students, but they are valuable references that will help you answer children's questions about this difficult issue.

For suggestions about concrete actions you and children can take to help birds, look to the very inexpensive booklet, *Citizen's Guide to Migratory Bird Conservation* (Cornell Laboratory of Ornithology, 1995) or the more in-depth *Bring Back the Birds: What You Can Do to Save Threatened Species* by Greenberg and Reaser (Stackpole Books, 1995).

The National Fish and Wildlife Foundation publishes a newsletter, *Partners in Flight,* rich with conservation information and educational projects about neotropical migrants. For information, write them at 1120 Connecticut Ave. NW, Suite 900, Washington, D.C. 20036.

## Words for birds

The Prothonotary Warbler takes its name from a papal notary whose ecclesiastical garb included a lemon-yellow hood. The Pileated Woodpecker's name comes from the Latin *pileum,* for a brimless skullcap worn by ancient Romans. Lewis and Clark were charged by President Thomas Jefferson to collect as many kinds of wildlife as they discovered on their expedition—Lewis' Woodpecker and Clark's Nutcracker are named for them. This kind of information is available in Terres's *Audubon Encyclopedia,* but for more details you may turn to Ernest A. Choate's *The Dictionary of American Bird Names,* revised by Raymond A. Paynter, Jr. (The Harvard Common Press, Boston, 1985.) This inexpensive little book provides the etymology and meanings of common and scientific names of all North American birds, along with very brief biographies of the people for whom birds are named (such as Lincoln's Sparrow—which was named for a young friend of Audubon's, not the Great Emancipator). This book would be suitable for junior high and older students.

Barbara and Richard Mearns's *Audubon to Xantus: The Lives of Those Commemorated in North American Bird Names* (Academic Press, 1992) has detailed, lengthy biographies about the people for whom birds are named. This one's for high school and above.

### Books about attracting birds

Carrol L. Henderson's *Wild About Birds: The D.N.R. Bird Feeding Guide* (Minnesota Department of Natural Resources, St. Paul, 1995) is one of the most comprehensive bird feeding guides ever written, with hints about attracting insect-eaters like warblers and flycatchers as well as typical seed- and suet-eating species. It's beautiful, with a multitude of color photos including ones of children feeding birds. Detailed plans for building both simple and complicated feeders are included, along with woodshop basics. (The bird-feeder plan in Appendix II is from *Wild About Birds*.)

John V. Dennis's *A Complete Guide to Birdfeeding* (Random House, New York, 1994) is a fine book with lots of recipes for goopy suet cakes. The title pretty much says it all. Dennis's *A Guide to Western Bird Feeding* (Bird Watcher's Digest Press, Marietta, Ohio, 1991) is geared to the special requirements of birds in the West.

Carrol L. Henderson's *Woodworking for Wildlife: Homes for Birds and Mammals*, Second Edition, (1992) and *Landscaping for Wildlife* (1987) (Minnesota Department of Natural Resources) both brim with sound information and practical suggestions for attracting wildlife in the Midwest. They include lovely photos, including many of children.

## Regional guides

Comprehensive ornithological treatises have been written about the birdlife in many states. In some cases these were written before 1950 and are now out of print, but they are still usually found in public libraries and are often available at used bookstores. Some of these old volumes have fascinating anecdotes and interesting historical information. Newer treatises such as Samuel Robbins's *Wisconsin Birdlife* (University of Wisconsin Press, Madison, 1991) are wonderful references. Ask at your public library if your state has such a book.

Many states have a "birder's guide" with detailed directions to the best places for birding and a complete listing of all species recorded in the state and your likelihood of finding each one. Birder's guides not only tell you where but also when to look for each bird. Area checklists don't provide details about specific locations, but they usually show seasonal abundance for each species. Try to obtain the regional guide and checklist for your state—they will help you discover the best places to bring kids. These resources are all listed and available from the American Birding Association—call A.B.A. Sales (1-800-634-7736) to find out if any are available for your region.

## Books about specific bird groups

Most children develop a favorite bird. Encouraging them to read about it while their interest is high builds reading skills as it satisfies curiosity. Libraries and bookstores have an almost endless array of bird books with at least one fine selection about virtually any species—listing all the choices would be prohibitive. One group of birds—raptors—holds such enormous appeal for so many kids, from the tiniest kindergartners to the most hormonally-charged adolescents, that I list a few excellent choices to nurture kids' understanding and love.

Brian K. Wheeler and William S. Clark's *A Photographic Guide to North American Raptors* (Academic Press, London, 1995) includes 377 color photographs of forty-two hawks, eagles, and falcons. The text is technical and limited to identification, but even kindergartners will love and learn from the photos. Pete Dunne, David Sibley, and Clay Sutton's *Hawks in Flight* (Houghton Mifflin Company, Boston, 1988) also covers just identification, but it has exquisite line drawings of flying hawks and a text rich in the kinds of details that appeal to older adolescents, such as "A Merlin is to a Kestrel what a Harley-Davidson motorcycle is to a scooter."

Clay Sutton and Patricia Taylor Sutton's *How to Spot Hawks and Eagles* (Chapters Publishing Ltd., Shelburne, Vermont, 1996) includes a wealth of practical hints about finding and enjoying raptors as well as identifying them. This book includes brief but detailed life history accounts and is written in a simple style that will be understandable to middle grade students.

For fascinating fictional stories about the lives of hawks, turn to Pete Dunne's *The Wind Masters*, (Houghton Mifflin, Boston, 1995). Dunne's rich prose, lyrical and whimsical by turns, will appeal to better readers from middle school up. The accurate detail, supported by the author's years of experience with hawks, will foster understanding even as the stories themselves nourish adolescent (as well as adult) imaginations.

## Charming children's books

These are my personal favorites. Librarians can supply you with many many more.

George, Jean Craighead. (Any title—she's wonderful!)
Hamerstrom, Frances. *Walk when the Moon is Full*
Hickman, Pamela M. *Bird Wise* (many great projects for kids)
McMillan, Bruce. Many great titles—my favorite is *Nights of the Pufflings*
Mowat, Farley. *Owls in the Family*
Seuss, Dr. *Horton Hatches the Egg, The Lorax*
White, E. B. *The Trumpet of the Swan*
Yolen, Jane. *Owl Moon*

# INDEX

Pfeifer-Hamilton Publishers produces quality gift books
celebrating the special beauty and unique lifestyle of the north country.

Laura Erickson
*For the Birds: An Uncommon Guide*

Marina Lachecki Herman, Ann Schimpf,
Joseph Passineau, and Paul Treuer
*Teaching Kids to Love the Earth*

Marina Lachecki and James Kasperson
*More Teaching Kids to Love the Earth*

Larry Weber
*Backyard Almanac*

Jerry Wilber
*Wit & Wisdom of the Great Outdoors*

Mark Stensaas
*Canoe Country Wildlife*
*Canoe Country Flora*

John Bates
*Trailside Botany*

Bob Cary
*Tales from Jackpine Bob*
*Root Beer Lady*

Sam Cook
*Up North*
*Quiet Magic*
*CampSights*

Call us toll free at 800-247-6789 for a complete catalog.

**Pfeifer-Hamilton Publishers**
210 West Michigan Duluth MN 55802-1908